PROPHETIC FUNCTIONS

Book 2 - The Prophetic Field Guide Series

Second Edition

COLETTE TOACH

www.ami-bookshop.com

PROPHETIC FUNCTIONS
Book 2 - The Prophetic Field Guide Series
Second Edition

ISBN-10: 1626640068
ISBN-13: 978-1-62664-006-1

Copyright © 2016 by Apostolic Movement International, LLC
All rights reserved
5663 Balboa Ave #416,
San Diego,
California 92111,
United States of America

1st Printing May 2015
2nd Edition April 2016

Published by **Apostolic Movement International, LLC**
E-mail Address: admin@ami-bookshop.com
Web Address: www.ami-bookshop.com

All rights reserved under International Copyright Law.
Contents may not be reproduced in whole or in part in any form without the express written consent of the publisher.

Unless specified, all Scripture references taken from the New King James Version®. Copyright © 1982 by Thomas Nelson. Used by permission. All rights reserved.

Contents

Contents 3

Introduction – Hearing God's Voice 8
    The Secret Weapon of the Prophet – Faith! 9
    God – the Master of Variety 12
    Seven Different Ways to Hear God 12

Chapter 01 – The Nature of Jesus 16
    What We are Ready to Hear 16
    The Nature of God 19
    Understanding What Rhema Is 22
    … As You are Known 24

Chapter 02 – Man as a Tripartite Being 30
    1. The Outer Court – The Body 32
    2. The Inner Court/Holy Place – The Soul 33
    3. The Holy of Holies – The Spirit 34
    The Functions of the Soul 35
    Your Five Senses 36
    When God Talks Back 38
    Relating it to the Urim and Thummim 39

Chapter 03 – Functioning in the Urim and Thummim . 42
    What to Do With It 45

Chapter 04 – Prophetic Dreams: Exploring Their Purpose 60

Three Main Prophetic Dream Groups 62
Prophetic Dreams: Exploring Their Purpose 63
Chapter 05 – The Skinny of Dream Categories 78
Prophetic Dreams – Why and When 84
The Missing Step 86
Chapter 06 – Character Specific and Universal Symbols 92
1. Giving Birth or Being Pregnant 94
2. Death 101
3. Crying in Your Sleep 103
4. Your House 104
5. Relatives 106
6. Dreaming of Flying 109
7. Hair 112
8. Key 114
At the End of the Day 116
Chapter 07 – 3 Prophetic Dream Groups 120
1. Personal Prophetic Dream 121
2. Prophetic Dream for the Church 122
3. Prophetic Dream for Others 124
Chapter 08 – Functioning in Visions 132
What's a Vision? 132
The Gentle Breeze of Jesus 134
Vision Types 135

The Three Vision Categories 137
Watching for Deception 145

Chapter 09 – Functioning in Tongues 150
The Language of the Spirit 151
Purpose of Speaking in Tongues 153
Uses for Speaking in Tongues 158

Chapter 10 – Functioning in Utterance and Interpretation 164
The Difference Between Utterance and Interpretation 165
How to Interpret Effectively 167
Learning to Flow in Utterance and Interpretation ... 168

Chapter 11 – Functioning in Prophecy 172
The Truth About Prophecy 173
Prophecy – Step 1 and 2 177

Chapter 12 – Breaking Prophecy Down 182
Prophecy and Faith 186
What to Do if God Does not Speak 189

Chapter 13 – General vs. Personal Prophecy 196
The General Prophecy 196

Chapter 14 – Functioning in Journaling 204
Do's and Don'ts of Journaling 208
Final Challenge 224

Chapter 15 – Functioning in the Audible and Still Small Voice 226
- The Audible Voice 226
- The Still Small Voice 229
- How Do You Know if It's God? 230
- Spiritual Maturity 232

Chapter 16 – The Sign of True Intimacy 238

About the Author 245

Recommendations by the Author 247
- Prophetic Anointing 247
- Presentation of Prophecy 247
- I'm Not Crazy - I'm a Prophet 248
- The Way of Dreams & Visions Book with Symbol Dictionary Kit 248
- Practical Prophetic Ministry 249
- Prophetic Essentials 249
- A.M.I. Prophetic School 250

Contact Information 251

INTRODUCTION

HEARING GOD'S VOICE

Introduction – Hearing God's Voice

> *Ephesians 3*
> *5 Which in other ages was not made known to the sons of men, as it has now been revealed by the Spirit to His holy apostles and prophets:*

Why is it that the Lord reveals His will to the prophets? From this page onwards, you will begin to understand yourself and your calling more than you ever have before. It is no secret that prophets receive unconscious revelation. You know very well that the prophet operates in the gift of prophecy and visions.

Have you ever asked yourself though what the point of it all was? What is the point of getting one revelation after another? What is the point of speaking one prophecy after another – especially when you do so without immediate fruit sometimes?

Well, that is what this book will begin to tackle from the first page. You see, there is a reason that it is essential for you to hear the voice of God. No, the primary reason is not to just make you look good in front of the Church.

Rather it is meant to impart something to you that the Church desperately lacks – Faith!

> *Romans 10*
> *17 So then faith comes by hearing, and hearing by the word of God.*

THE SECRET WEAPON OF THE PROPHET – FAITH!

Faith comes when we hear the rhema word of God. I have seen people read the Scriptures for years, but still panic when they are faced with a simple head cold! How are we, as prophets, going to mature the Church if we cannot even give them faith and hope for their daily struggles?

Well, that is where you come in. Let's rewind a little bit and look at all our heroes of faith. We have King David, Gideon, Samson and Elijah. Each one of them was a mighty warrior in their own right.

What always amazed me, as I read of their feats, was the boldness they had when God gave them an instruction. God told Elijah to have a face-off with the prophets of Baal, and without any fear for his own life, he went and did it.

Then after all was said and done, it felt as if the "flesh" suddenly kicked in. After performing such miracles, we see that same Elijah running for the hills in fear of Jezebel. What happened here?

RHEMA EMPOWERS US WITH FAITH

What happened is that when God spoke to Elijah – faith was imparted with that rhema word! This faith gave Elijah all the boldness he needed to get the job done. After the job was done though, he failed to get another rhema word on what to do next.

We see him running to the desert and from here the Lord appears to Him again – this time through the still small voice. The result? Faith!

Faith is the weapon in your hand to make things happen. Wouldn't it be wonderful to know without a doubt, that when you speak a decree, that it will come to pass?

Wouldn't it be wonderful if you went into a meeting, knowing that God will arrive with all His power and anointing? Well, all you need, to make these things happen is… faith!

So then we come to our million-dollar question, "How do I get this faith?" It is quite easy actually. I have taught a lot on the subject of faith in my teaching, *Progressive Faith – the Power to Make Things Happen*, but I want to look at the subject as it relates to the prophet specifically.

The truth is you need faith to make things happen in your ministry. You need faith to remove the obstacles that stand in the way of you doing what God has called you to do.

You need faith and boldness to stand up and say what needs to be said – even if those words are not what others want to hear.

You need… the power to make things happen!

KEY PRINCIPLE

> Faith comes by hearing the rhema word of God.

Is the principle beginning to sink into your spirit yet? If you want the kind of faith that makes things happen when you minister – then you need to hear the rhema word of God!

When you hear the rhema word of God, it brings with it the faith you need to take action. This is why the Lord keeps drawing you into a close relationship with Him. It is so that you can hear His voice.

Unfortunately though, so many prophets get all caught up on "visions" and "prophecies" that they overlook the function of each. There is a reason that God gives us visions. There is a reason why He speaks in dreams!

He is trying to give you His rhema word! He is trying to build your faith. So that is exactly what I am going to train you to do in this book.

I am going to train you to hear the rhema word of God and then to act on that rhema, to cause things to happen in your ministry. From there, you will be able to take that same measure of faith and use it to see results in those that you minister to!

GOD – THE MASTER OF VARIETY

I love that the Lord is so versatile. He must have been pretty sure of Himself when He created expressives such as myself, because along with my temperament, He also created different ways to keep me interested!

I say this, because being expressive, I tend to get bored of doing things the same way all the time. I like exploring new things.

Well, the Lord is no different! When it comes to speaking to us, He understands where we are. He knows what will reach us and *how* we need to hear that rhema word. All we need to do is to open our ears to hear it.

So you can rest assured that there is no single way to hear that rhema word. In fact, as you might already have known, there are at least 7 ways to hear His rhema word right now!

If you are not able to hear Him in one way, He is waiting to show you another! In this book I am going to tackle just 7 ways to hear His voice. I have covered other ways in a different teaching, but I wanted to pick out the ways that He speaks specifically to the prophet… *you*!

SEVEN DIFFERENT WAYS TO HEAR GOD

I challenge you to become as versatile as the Lord is. If you are comfortable with hearing His voice in one way, challenge yourself to hear Him in other ways. I know how easy it is to slip into a comfort zone and to restrict God to one way of talking.

Would you do that to someone you love? Imagine how boring my marriage would be if I could only hear my husband when he spoke in a whisper?

Instead, we communicate with one another in so many different ways.

So let's take a look at the different ways you can hear God's voice, and I am hoping that as you go through each one, that they spark off a fresh experience between you and the Lord.

Here are seven ways that you will learn to hear the Lord!

1. Through Urim and Thummim
2. Dreams
3. Visions
4. Tongues and Interpretation
5. Prophecy
6. Journaling
7. The Still Small Voice

I pray that each one is chili pepper in your life to bring a newfound passion to your relationship with the Lord.

KEY PRINCIPLE

To keep things alive in any relationship, it helps to add some "spice!" By learning to hear the voice of God in every way possible, you will find a new "zing" added to your spiritual life!

CHAPTER 01

THE NATURE OF JESUS

Chapter 01 – The Nature of Jesus

There are very few people who communicate directly and say exactly what they feel. For the most part you have to "pick up" what they feel through body language or through subtle suggestion.

Despite the occasional hothead, learning to understand people is fun! Learning to hear what they are *not* saying makes you a better listener! In fact, take any relationship in your life right now, and determine how you communicate with that person.

Do you always say what you think or feel outright? Do you blurt out everything you think 24 hours a day? Why not? Well, to be truthful, that person is just not ready to hear what you have to say sometimes.

What We are Ready to Hear

I remember when Craig and I were first married and we were still learning the ropes of what it meant to be husband and wife. There were some things that he did in our marriage that I was not comfortable with.

The thing is, I could see how hard he was trying to impress me. I knew that if I just smashed what he was doing, that it would hurt him and make him feel insecure. So I did what any other woman would do... I hinted!

I would hint at doing something else instead of the thing he thought I would like. It took some time for us to get comfortable with one another and the day came when we knew each other so well that I could say, "Love, the truth is... I really do not like that particular thing you do. I know you think I like it, but I really do not."

Of course he asked, " Well, why didn't you tell me?"

"Well, if I had told you in the moment when you were feeling vulnerable, would you really have been open to hear it?"

"Probably not!"

Now what has this dialog got to do with hearing the voice of God? Whether you like to believe it or not, we are quite a sensitive bunch.

WALKING ON EGGSHELLS AROUND THE PROPHET!

Prophets especially, have faced so much rejection through life that there are things that make them run for cover. The Lord is very mindful of that. I have worked with enough prophets who confess, "Correct me! Shape me! I am ready!" Only to discover instead that, these are the ones, that call for me to "walk on eggshells" when the pressure comes. They are not as strong as they think they are!

The Lord knows that there are hurts, fears and strengths in each of us that need to be handled differently. That is why He chooses to talk to each one of us in a way that is best for us.

KEY PRINCIPLE

> The Lord will approach you according to the way you are able to hear Him right now.

He treats us like in the illustration I shared of Craig and I. He knows that there are things we are doing that need change. He knows that there are some things we need to do, that we are not ready to do yet.

He knows that there is flesh that must go, that we are not ready to face. He knows of the pride that must be brought to the cross.

He knows the bitterness in our hearts that we have harbored jealously for years. He even knows how we deny these sins and try to tuck them away, so that no one can see them.

He is a tender groom and He is not going to deal with all of these things at the same time! Rather, He is going to start where you are at and speak to you in a way that you will understand, right now.

THE NATURE OF GOD

As you come to know more of His nature and realize that even when He is correcting you, that it is in love, He will change the way He talks.

When you first date someone, you try to put on your best appearance. Yes, you want the person to see who you are, but you and I both know that they are not ready to see *everything* about you on that first date!

Certain flaws and weaknesses can wait for a time when you know the person better. Well, that is how the Lord treats you and I as well. He does not just "rush" you and expose things that He knows very well you are not ready to admit.

He will not shout at you and make a demand for something that He knows very well you will not do. Rather, He woos you. This is the nature of your Savior. You will come to know Him through the various ways He speaks.

That is the kind of nature that Isaiah was trying to get across to us in the following passage:

> *Isaiah 42*
> *3 A bruised reed He will not break, and smoking flax He will not quench; He will bring forth justice for truth.*

The Secret to Knowing

He will not try to "break a bruised reed" or "quench a smoking flax!" Rather He will handle the situation delicately and bring forth the judgment that you need, through a truth you are able to receive.

And so, when it comes to hearing God's rhema word, He will speak to you in a way that you are most comfortable hearing. This might be through dreams, or perhaps He will speak through visions.

Ask yourself, "How do I hear the Lord the most?"

The chances are, that this is "home" for you. It is where you are most comfortable and what you had a good experience with. The thing is, you can only go deeper into any relationship when you get to know every aspect of a person's nature.

Now, the Lord has been patient with you and He has spoken to you as you prefer to hear, but are you taking Him into consideration? Are you allowing Him to lead you into a deeper knowledge of Him?

> *1 Corinthians 13*
> *12 For now we see in a mirror, dimly, but then face to face. Now I know in part, but then I shall know just as I also am known.*
> *13 And now abide faith, hope, love, these three; but the greatest of these is love.*

How exactly do you gain that deeper knowledge? How do you know Him as well as He knows you? Well, when you apply this scripture here in 1 Corinthians 13:12, you begin to know all aspects of His nature. You begin to hear His voice from every perspective of who He is!

This is not something unknown to you. Go back to a close relationship you have with a spouse or a friend. I am going to use my husband as an example, because I love how the marriage relationship perfectly illustrates our relationship with the Lord Jesus.

To Know and be Known

Craig and I married in 1995 and it took us a good few years to get to know one another. Just when I got to know one aspect of my husband's nature, the Lord threw us into a new set of circumstances and I got to see another side altogether.

The husband I knew when everything was going well, was not exactly the same as the one that lost his job during the recession in our country. The man who was always as cool as a cucumber, showed a new nature altogether, when he was faced with the cares of trying to feed two small babies. All the while trying to feel like he was being a good husband to me!

Allowing Relationships to Evolve

When we first married, he would hint or speak gently to me. When the pressure was on, I found that he could also be very direct. Sure, I did not always like it, but in those moments I got to know him a bit better. The more experiences we had in life, the more we found that there were so many parts to who we were as individuals and as a couple that were hidden.

He got to see my "angry" face more than once. He got to see me giggle like a schoolgirl. He got to hear me be direct. He got to see me be gentle. Now, after years of marriage, he can just look at me and tell from my body language what I am thinking!

Imagine being able to do that with the Lord. Well, that is what this long illustration is all about! You see, you know how to hear the Lord in one way, but what if you could know every aspect of His nature so well, that you could know what He was thinking just from the slightest move of the spirit?

UNDERSTANDING WHAT RHEMA IS

I have gone on a bit now about how the rhema word of the Lord produces faith. What does "rhema" mean exactly? Let me borrow the wits of a fantastic man by the name of James Strong who put together one of the greatest bible study tools of our time – the *Strong's Concordance*.

Here is his take on the direct translation of the word "Rhema" as it is used in the original Greek text of the New Testament:

> 4487 rhema {hray'-mah}
>
> 1) that which is or has been uttered by the living voice, thing spoken, word

1a) any sound produced by the voice and having definite meaning
1b) speech, discourse
   1b1) what one has said
1c) a series of words joined together into a sentence (a declaration of one's mind made in words)
   1c1) an utterance

So when Romans 10 tells us that faith comes by hearing and hearing by the rhema word of God, it is saying the following:

Faith comes by hearing, and hearing by the utterance of the Lord as He gives it to you for a situation, right now!

The rhema Word of God is a speech, word, utterance or concept that the Lord is revealing to you right now. It is a living word. So no, it is not good enough to live off the revelations and words the Lord told you yesterday or last year.

If you want faith, then you need your rhema for today. There is no better way to receive that, than having your spiritual ears open to hear His voice from day to day! Apostle Paul certainly "got it."

Did you ever wonder how he could "pray without ceasing?" Well, he was not just doing all the talking. He was doing a lot of listening too, so that he could hear God's rhema word and act on it in perfect time.

Clarity in Rhema Produces Faith

When you can hear Him in this way, you will have faith to move mountains. You will not doubt what you hear from Him. You will not fear what man can do to you. You will not wonder, "Did I miss it?"

Above all, you will mature more spiritually with each rhema word you are able to receive. So firstly, passionately embrace the idea of being able to know God in every aspect of His nature.

Be flexible in how you hear His voice, so that you can come to the place in your relationship, where He can tell you what He wants to – and you are ready to receive it!

Above all, when you learn to hear His voice, be mindful of the portion of faith that He will give you along with it. From there, take that faith and use it to make things happen!

... As You are Known

Before you can even begin experiencing the full nature of God, it is a pretty good idea to start with knowing yourself. Just like our passage in Corinthians suggests, the Lord Jesus wants to take us to a place where we know Him as well as He knows us.

It stands to reason then, that knowing yourself would also be a good investment of knowledge and understanding. In the prophetic books I have written up until now, I have surrounded teaching with prophetic inspiration.

I am going to change things up a bit here and bring the teaching of the prophetic ministry more to the fore and then leave additional inspiration for the book that follows this one.

By the time you are done reading, I want to have accomplished the following things in you:

- To know how the Lord created you
- Understand how the Lord speaks to you
- Know why the Lord speaks to you
- Grasp the mechanics of how the realm of the spirit works
- Fully comprehend the power and authority of the word when it is spoken forth with faith
- How to gain that faith and so increase prophetic authority
- To function as a prophet, not just in deed, but in wisdom and understanding as well

BECOME FULLY EQUIPPED

As you can see, we have a lot of ground to cover. It is probably not the wisest practice to attempt to teach prophets doctrine, but then I am reminded that at this phase of your training, you have moved past the euphoria of prophetic ministry, and are ready to get down to business.

When you are approached about the "why" of how to hear the Lord, or when you are approached about the "why" a decree does or does not work, I want you to have the answer.

This book is not so much about imparting spiritual gifts to you, as much as it is about equipping you to do your job! I want to equip you in spirit, soul, and body!

I do not just want you to flow in the gifts of revelation, but I want you to be able to explain why they work. Know why the Lord chooses to use prophets in this way.

So you might find yourself reading through this and putting it on your bookshelf as a textbook for future reference. I will be referencing a lot more Scripture than I usually do.

Sure, I cannot teach without trying to inspire you, but for the chapters that are about to follow, make no mistake – I want to train you!

I want you to live the following passage:

> *2 Timothy 3*
> *16 All Scripture is given by inspiration of God, and is profitable for doctrine, for reproof, for correction, for instruction in righteousness,*
> *17 that the man of God may be complete, thoroughly equipped for every good work.*

It is time for you to become equipped to do good works of every kind. If you are to fulfill the function of a prophet in the Church today, there are a few things you need to learn.

Revelation alone is not going to take you there. Knowledge alone is not going to take you there. What we need to do is combine both of these and cause you to grow up.

You will come to a place in your prophetic ministry where the prophetic words will feel repetitive. There will come a time when all you know are principles!

A LINE IN THE SAND

The following chapters are a line in the sand between mediocrity and a journey towards prophetic maturity.

So allow me to bring you to maturity by introducing you… to yourself! Once you understand how the Lord has made you, you will understand why He speaks to you the way that He does.

From there, you will grasp why others think the way that they do as well. This will be another tool in your prophetic belt that will assist you in a successful ministry. For now though, let's begin your first workout.

Head off to the starting line of the race and wait for the gun to go off as we head towards understanding what makes you tick!

CHAPTER 02

MAN AS A TRIPARTITE BEING

Chapter 02 – Man as a Tripartite Being

I love a good debate and it does not get any better when you start studying on how man is made up! When it comes to our spirit and soul there is a lot of debate in the Church regarding this doctrine.

Some believe that man is made up of soul and body only. Their doctrinal viewpoint is that our spirit and soul are one entity. Others (myself included) believe that man is made up of three distinct parts. These parts are the spirit, soul and body.

When you look at the creation so far, this makes sense to me. Especially when you look at the progression of God's creation.

> *Genesis 1*
> *27 So God created man in His own image; in the image of God He created him; male and female He created them.*

My personal conviction though, comes from the simplicity of the fact that we are created in the image of God. If you look at the nature of God and how He is made up, you see that He is also a tripartite being. God consists of Father, Son, and Holy Spirit.

Each is distinct, yet all are the same. You cannot touch the Father without touching the Son. You cannot touch the Son, without touching the Holy Spirit. Each is so distinct and has their own function, yet they are not three gods - they are one!

I found this doctrine so easy to understand when I realized that I have been made in the image of God!

KEY PRINCIPLE

> Man is made up of spirit, soul and body.

If you touch my body, you are touching me! If you touch my spirit, you are touching me! Each part is so distinct with distinct functions. However, they make me completely one.

Doesn't that bring the picture together for you? If my spirit had to leave my body, I would surely die, because it is who I am. Yet, when you break it down, you see that man has clear functions that are made from a pattern originating from the image of God Himself.

> *1 Thessalonians 5 (KJV)*
> *23 And the very God of peace sanctify you wholly; and [I pray God] your whole spirit and soul and body be preserved blameless unto the coming of our Lord Jesus Christ.*

This passage speaks of getting your spirit, soul and body in line. There is no greater illustration of this in the Word than that of the tabernacle.

As you well know, the Word says that we are the temple of the Lord. This again confirms the fact that we are tripartite - because the temple had three distinct parts!

Let us look at each of these right now.

1. THE OUTER COURT – THE BODY

The first part of the tabernacle was called the Outer Court. This is the part where any Israelite could come and bring their offerings to God. It was public, just as our bodies are public. It is the part of ourselves that shows the world who we are. It is what people first come to know as "us". However, this is only the start of any relationship.

Just as the Outer Court had clear functions – so do our bodies! In fact, if you had to sum up three natural functions of the body they would read like this key principle.

KEY PRINCIPLE

> The functions of the body are:
> a. Nourishment
> b. Self Defense
> c. Reproduction

As the saying goes, "beauty is only skin deep" and so who we truly are is not reflected by how we look. Who we are lies in the seat of our soul!

2. THE INNER COURT/HOLY PLACE – THE SOUL

The second part of the Tabernacle was called the Inner Court or Holy Place. It was an area that only the priests could enter. Not just any Joe could walk in and do what they wanted. Even then the priests had to fulfill certain conditions before they could enter. They had to be ceremonially clean and had to wash before coming into this part of the Temple.

This is a fantastic picture of our souls, because this part shows who we are, and we restrict it to a certain few. Only those who are allowed close enough, truly get to know you. Here lies your mind, emotions, and will. Your soul is a bridge between your body and spirit. It is also the control tower that decides what it will let through.

Your soul is where you make the decision to obey your spirit, or to follow after the things of your flesh! The Scripture says that we are to diffuse the fragrance of Christ wherever we go - it is no surprise then, that the Altar of Incense could be found in the Holy Place. What we say, do or think, reflects what is in our spirits.

Either this can be a fragrance that diffuses Christ, or it can be the smell of rotting flesh. Either way, your soul makes these choices. (2 Corinthians 2:14)

Just like your body, your soul also has three distinct functions. Make a good note of them because I will refer to them very often throughout this book.

KEY PRINCIPLE

> The functions of the soul are:
> a. Mind
> b. Emotions
> c. Will

---

3. THE HOLY OF HOLIES – THE SPIRIT

The Holy of Holies of the tabernacle contained the Ark of the Covenant and only the High Priest could enter into it. It was the most holy place and it was where God sat upon His "throne." It was where the cloud rested. It is a beautiful picture of our human spirits and what God intended for us.

As a human being, God has given us as a spirit. However as a Christian, your spirit becomes His throne! It becomes a place where the cloud of God rests. Understanding this concept makes you realize everything that is available to us as believers!

Not only do we have a spirit that can communicate with the Lord, but it is a place that contains His power as well. What miracles are you looking for today? Do you realize that Jesus is on your throne? He is seated in your spirit and He has brought along with Him all the authority that Adam lost.

It means that at the name of Jesus every demon must bow! When you realize that the power of God is not something you have to run after, but something that is within you, it brings you peace and builds your faith.

You already know the functions of both the body and soul – but how about the spirit?

KEY PRINCIPLE

The functions of the spirit are:
a. Intuition
b. Communion
c. Spirit of Wisdom/Foreknowledge

As you get a full picture of how God made you, you will also start to see the vast authority you now have in Christ. You do not need to wander through life, waiting for something to happen to you. Rather, you can know who you are, know who the Lord is, and rest in that power!

THE FUNCTIONS OF THE SOUL

Although the study of man is fascinating, I want to look specifically at the soul, because this is the part that God uses the most when He speaks to you through Urim and Thummim.

You face stimuli every day. If you think back on your day so far, you might remember the taste of your bagel. Perhaps you remember the smell of cigarette smoke on the way to your office and the sound of honking of horns as you got stuck in traffic.

Everywhere you go, stimuli are being fed into your spirit via your soul. Now although a lot of that can be negative, a lot is positive as well. For example, each time you read the Word or experience the anointing, you are feeding it into your spirit.

Key Principle

> So the pattern looks a little bit like this:
> Sensation on the body > Creates a thought/emotion in the soul >
> Leaves an impression on your spirit!

Your Five Senses

Everything you see, taste, touch, smell or hear through your body has an effect on your soul! It affects your mind (the way you think). It makes you feel something in your emotions, or it drives your will to action.

This is the way God created us, and it helps us sort through everything we receive. We accumulate all the information around us through the five senses in our bodies. It is our soul that makes sense of it so that we can "get a handle" on everything that is going on around us.

It is our God-given ability that assists us in learning. A baby falls, and the pain compels him to balance better. The same baby tastes candy for the first time, and it compels him to ask for more… bit by bit our soul makes sense of everything we experience throughout our day.

From there, it creates templates for life. Now use this in a spiritual context and you have a bomb of potential! Each time you allow yourself to experience things in the Word and spirit of God, you feed that influence into your soul, creating a solid foundation in your spirit!

This is what Paul meant when he said,

> *Romans 12*
> *2 And do not be conformed to this world, but be transformed by the renewing of your mind, that you may prove what is that good and acceptable and perfect will of God.*

By allowing the spirit of God to dominate your senses, it will change the way you think, allowing you to know the will of God!

That is why I teach the prophets to meditate on the Word and to visualize it – so that they can create good spiritual templates for life.

When God Talks Back

Now when God talks back to you, He is going to use the same modus operandi. He is going to use your mind, emotions and will, to get His message across to you. Just like the world imposes its will on you daily, from your body inwards, the Lord will speak gently to you in your spirit. What He says in your spirit can then be expressed outward.

The same way our soul comprehends stimuli through the five senses fed through our bodies - the Lord will speak through those same senses again from the spirit! He will feed you information that you can taste, touch, smell, feel or hear!

Think about that for a moment. You might be in a church meeting when you will suddenly feel a deep peace enter your heart. You might even taste or smell something in the spirit. Sometimes these impressions are so strong that you might even smell or taste it physically!

The Mind – A One Way Street

Now, it is important to keep in mind that you cannot take stimuli in and express them outwardly all at the same time. Your mind tends to be a one-way street. Have you noticed how hard it is to hear the gentle promptings from the Spirit when you are distracted with noise round about you?

That is why it is important to take time to feed into your spirit and just as important, to stop for a moment, to listen to what the Lord is saying deep inside of you. When you need to hear the Lord, try cutting out the distractions around you. Turn down the music and shut out the noise.

If you feel uncomfortable, find a better chair to sit on.

Quiet those senses of yours for a little while, so that you can feel the Lord trying to express Himself through them from within.

RELATING IT TO THE URIM AND THUMMIM

Well, this is, in essence how the Urim and Thummim work. It is simply God speaking through your spirit and influencing the emotions in your soul.

The Lord speaks specifically through the "emotion function" of your soul when giving you a Urim or Thummim. When He speaks to you in this way, you will experience a deep gut feeling of "YES!" or one of "NO!"

Now that you understand the concept, how can you begin using this powerful tool right now? Well, that is exactly what I have in store for you in the next chapter. So put down your notes and get ready to make the theory you just learned, practical.

CHAPTER 03

USING THE URIM AND THUMMIM PRACTICALLY

Chapter 03 – Functioning in the Urim and Thummim

> *Exodus 28*
> *30 And you shall put in the breastplate of judgment the Urim and the Thummim, and they shall be over Aaron's heart when he goes in before the Lord. So Aaron shall bear the judgment of the children of Israel over his heart before the Lord continually.*

In the Old Testament, the Lord had Moses make a very special robe for Aaron to wear during his office. By far the most fascinating part of it, was the breastplate. You can read all the details of it in Exodus 28, but I want to draw your attention to the mentioned Urim and Thummim.

Key Principle

> The Urim and Thummim were two objects inserted into the High Priest's breastplate that provided a "yes" or "no" answer from God.

Tradition suggests that they were two smooth stones – one being black and the other white. So depending on which one Aaron pulled out, would give you the direct answer from God that you needed.

Functioning in the Urim and Thummim

You will see this mentioned a number of times in the Old Testament and it was a wonderful way for the children of Israel to get a direct answer from the Lord.

When they needed a "yes" or "no" answer about something, they would pay Aaron a visit. He would then slip his hand into his breastplate and pull out either the "Urim" or the "Thummim."

Getting a Urim from the Lord said "yes" and a Thummim said "no!" Wouldn't it be nice to have a set of these stones hanging around in your sock drawer for emergencies? Well, the good news is that we have something way better than that.

From the time the Holy Spirit came to dwell inside of you, He brought along His Urim and Thummim and deposited them directly into your spirit. Aaron wore the stones over his heart – a symbol of what we now have through Christ. We now have our own inheritance inside our hearts!

> *Ephesians 6*
> *14 Stand therefore, having girded your waist with truth, having put on the breastplate of righteousness.*

Today, every believer gets to wear the breastplate! With the indwelling of the Holy Spirit, comes the ability to get a straight answer from the Lord.

Knowing the "Yes" and "No"

So how does it work? To get a full understanding of how God speaks to us, you will need to know a bit about the nature of man.

I will give you a quick breakdown, to help you see exactly how the Lord speaks to us, starting of course, with the Urim and Thummim. In the last chapter, I gave you a quick summary of how man is made up.

Pinpointing the times that the Lord spoke to you using the Urim and Thummim is easier than you think. In fact, by the time I am finished, you will sit back with a sigh of relief, knowing that you have been hearing Him all along. You might not have recognized it, but that does not mean He was not speaking!

Just think back on some life changing experiences. I guarantee that during these times you either had a deep sense of peace or a deep sense of foreboding. Well, that was your Urim and Thummim talking there.

The Lord was giving you the "yes/no" answer you were looking for. In fact, once you make it a practice to listen to the influence from your spirit more often, you will come to realize that you get these deep feelings throughout your day.

LISTENING TO YOUR SPIRIT

The key to the Urim and Thummim is to be sensitive to the Spirit. I think that especially with us prophets, we run ahead of the Lord sometimes.

Our mind gets in the way, and we get an idea of what we should be doing. Before the Lord has had a chance to speak to us, we are off... We are doing, making and we are changing the world. It is only when we hit that big fat wall that we come to realize, "Actually, I should have listened to my spirit."

This is something that you should be developing on a daily basis. What is fantastic about the spiritual Urim and Thummim is that this is something that you can do 24 hours a day, because the Holy Spirit is speaking 24 hours a day.

He is telling you where to go and what direction to take in every part of your life.

Don't sit and wait for the Urim and Thummim only when you are ministering or when you need specific direction. What I want you to do now is to be aware of the Urim and Thummim in your spirit all of the time and for every decision that you make.

WHAT TO DO WITH IT

In the introduction, I shared how hearing the rhema word of God produces faith. As you learn to develop this way of hearing what God has to say, you will become bolder in acting on that word.

Here is a truth to hold on to though:

KEY PRINCIPLE

> A rhema word will fall flat if it is not followed by an act of faith!

What is the point of the Lord prompting you, if you never act on that prompting? The only time you will see things happen in your ministry, is when you not only hear that rhema word, but act on it as well.

How many times have you failed to do this? You are going about your daily business and sense a nudging in your spirit to go somewhere, or to take a certain turn. You do not follow that nudging. You end up in trouble.

Later on you say to yourself, " I should have obeyed my spirit!" It is only when we move forward in faith, that we see the fruition of this promise:

> *Isaiah 55*
> *11 So shall My word be that goes forth from My mouth; it shall not return to Me void, but it shall accomplish what I please, and it shall prosper in the thing for which I sent it.*

So just when you get used to the idea that you need a rhema word from the Lord to increase your faith, you need to move on to realizing that if you do not apply that word, nothing will happen.

Suddenly all the times your prophetic words did not come to pass… make sense. The more we look at the various ways that the Lord can give you His rhema word, the more you realize that each time He talks, that He usually follows up that promise with an instruction.

When you feel a Urim or Thummim in the spirit, the Lord expects you to do something about it. He is not sharing this bit of conversation with you just for your interest.

If you are ministering to someone and you feel a Thummim about praying with them, then the Lord expects you to stop and not pray!

If you are in intercession and you feel a Urim when you bring someone before the Lord, then He expects you to pray for that person.

When you perform that simple step of obedience, you will find your conversations with the Lord becoming more frequent as He tells you more.

PROGRESSIVE CONVERSATION

What will begin as a Urim and Thummim to get your attention, will progress towards visions, dreams, tongues, utterance and the still small voice!

The more you are obedient to one form of the Lord's voice, the more you will be able to hear Him through the other ways.

So although the Urim and Thummim seems like the most basic way of hearing His voice, consider it a platform that has the potential to propel you to new heights in the spirit, that you have not entered into before.

We all need to begin somewhere! If you cannot even be obedient to the Urim and Thummim you sense each day – then how can the Lord entrust you with greater revelations?

If my son is not even able to recite the alphabet, how can I try to make him read a full book? Yes I know… we prophets are impatient. You want the Lord to speak to you right now like He did with Moses. You want this passage to be a reality in your life:

> *Exodus 33*
> *11 So the Lord spoke to Moses face to face, as a man speaks to his friend…*

That is most certainly your goal as a prophet, but if you cannot even follow "yes" or "no" instructions, how will your ear hear when the Lord tells you to do something that you really do not want to do?

BRING IT ON HOME!

So let's bring this subject right on home! I know that by now you are well aware of how the Urim and Thummim works. We have labored the point regarding this subject in so many other books.

However, instead of just looking at the times when you sensed the Urim or Thummim, I want you to challenge yourself instead.

How about looking at the times that you disobeyed that prompting? I am sure that you do not need to think very far back, to remember a time you felt a caution in your spirit, but plowed through anyway!

Or a time when you felt that you needed to say something, but fear got the better of you and you went away "holding it all in."

It is easy to be aware of the times when God speaks in this manner, but let me draw your attention to the action that should follow this rhema word.

CONSIDER THESE CASE SCENARIOS IF YOU WILL:

THE "I HAD YOU ON MY HEART" SCENARIO

You sit down to write an e-mail or letter to someone and as you begin to write, you feel uncertain in your spirit. You find the words difficult to get out, and although you know what you need to say, you still have this nagging thought at the back of your mind, that you should wait.

On the other side, you feel bad because you have not written in a while. The person has been nagging you and saying, "You have not written to me! What is wrong? When are you going to write?"

And so although you feel that caution (Thummim) you push through anyway. Obligation trumps the Thummim and you send off your little note.

Is it any surprise that the words you wrote did not hit their mark? Now you might have given some good counsel. Perhaps you even said nice things. At the end of the day though, did your words carry the faith, imparted through the rhema from God?

No, you sent out soulish words. Those were words taken from your own wisdom. Sure, you will not ruin the world as you know it, but you will not see things happen because of it. The best that could happen is… nothing! The worst that could happen is, that you get a negative response and realize you just wasted your time!

On the flip side of this scenario, you sit down to do some work and a friend pops into your mind. You feel this gentle nudging that says, "Why not just drop them a quick line."

You take another look at your workload and think to yourself, "That is a good idea! Let me just get this other stuff out of the way first and then I will get to it…"

Throughout the day, that same nudging comes, but you put it aside for more "urgent" matters. The day passes and you do not write. Here, you missed that Urim! As it turns out, that person was going through a hard time and was crying out to God saying, "Lord, I really need to hear from you right now!"

It sounds a bit lame to say after the fact, "Oh yes! I thought something was up with you the other day. The Lord put you on my heart and I was really thinking about you…" That is like closing the barn door after the horse has bolted!

They do not need to hear after their crisis that "you had them on your heart." They need to hear words of power in their situation right now. To be truthful, when you say, "I had you on my heart", what you are really saying is, "I did think about you. In fact, the Holy Spirit really did put you on my heart – but I was too busy to act on that rhema word!"

Do you see how vital listening to the Lord in this way is? Seeing powerful results in your ministry is so simple.

KEY PRINCIPLE

> Just listen to that Urim and Thummim. Then act on it!

You will never be stuck doing things in the wrong timing again!

THE "I REALLY NEED A WORD" SCENARIO

Someone comes to you for prayer. Either they visit you personally, or they are attending one of your seminars. You know this person. They are having a hard time. They are crying out to the Lord for a breakthrough.

Your heart goes out to them and you know that the Lord wants to answer their prayer. You join hands to pray with them and get…. nothing!

Instead of a vision or direction, you get this uneasy feeling that the Lord does not want you to pray for them right now! Now you are on the spot! I know just how you feel.

When we host a graduation for our students or have a seminar, where I know that the Lord will appoint someone to a ministry office, I feel the fire of pressure, burning on me. I see the attendees looking at me, praying and hoping that the Lord will place them in office.

This is especially true of those who have spent years going through our training school. They feel ready and wait for that appointment. They come up and I get…. nothing! The Lord says, "Not now. They are not ready!"

How humiliating! Many others in the class were appointed. The Lord had so much to say to everyone else. You are on the stage. Everyone is looking. Everyone is expecting something and you get… nothing!

You feel uncomfortable, because surely, if you are a prophet or apostle, you should be able to twist the hand of God, right? When I first entered into prophetic office years ago, I will admit in shame that I failed more than once.

I tried to "wash away" the Thummim I felt by convincing myself that, "This person is surely ready! Look how much they have done for the Lord. I am sure that I am just making up this feeling of caution!"

The result? I might have laid hands and spoken words of, "I appoint you…" but nothing ever became of that person. In fact, I stole from them the opportunity to be tested! As difficult as the rejection might have been, in front of everyone, it would also have been just the training they needed to truly qualify for the office that God had for them.

So I will not judge you if you have failed. However, I will challenge you to learn to stand in the firing line! It has been many years since the Lord gave me the conviction to speak only what He tells me, and to obey what He prompts me to do.

Yes, I have received more than one backlash from those who felt cheated out of their appointment. What can we do? Should we please God or man?

Your Urim and Thummim is a tower for you to run to, to keep high above danger! Listen to it and apply it. It will save your skin more times than you can count.

THE "SHOULD I REALLY SAY THIS" SCENARIO

You find yourself in a conflict with someone: a pastor, spouse, friend or neighbor. The tensions have risen and it is high time that they got to hear what you *really* have to say!

You have been bottling up your hurt, thoughts and frustration for so long and now that this conflict is out in the open, you see it as an opportunity from the Lord to say what really needs to be said. (In your opinion anyway!)

So you let 'er rip! Just before you open your big prophetic jaw though, you feel a twinge in the pit of your stomach. You feel that Thummim in your spiritual breastplate, doubling up as a thorn in your flesh!

"Don't do it!"

"But I must say something or I will burst!"

"Don't do it!"

"It is about time that they really hear the truth… "

"I am telling you – don't do it!"

Slap this scenario into cartoon form and all of us can see a sketch of an angel on your right shoulder and a devil with a pitchfork on the other, as they both struggle to convince you to make the right decision.

We both know what decision you make, because, "This has been a long time coming!"

You push against your better judgment and say what you feel justified to say. Backlash. More arguing. The fight is extended another hour. If you are really blessed, the person just gets mad at you and walks out.

Now you know you missed it. You know that now was not the time to bring it up, yet you console yourself saying, "Well, it had to come out sooner or later, it may as well have been now!"

Perhaps that is true. Perhaps what you said did need to come out, but did it need to come out right now? Could there not have been a better time to share it? Say… when the person was actually open to listen?

Listening to your Urim and Thummim can save your marriage. It can save your relationships and in the end, save you a lot of grey hairs! How many times have you pushed yourself into hot water? The Lord came to save you. Sure, He came to save us from our sin, but honestly, sometimes I feel like He came to save us from ourselves even more!

Listen to the Lord speaking to you. He knows what that person needs to hear and when. Let Him make the judgment call instead of taking things into your hands.

THE "SHOULD WE INVEST INTO THIS" SCENARIO

This scenario is not directly related to your prophetic training, but does bear weight and is worthy of mention. As you learn to listen to these promptings in your spiritual life, you will recognize very quickly that the Lord is speaking in your natural life as well.

This is especially true when it comes to spending time or money on something important. We live in a society of "investment." Everyone wants to invest their time and money into something that is going to get the best results. It is so tempting to follow the trends of the world and what everyone else is doing.

A good case is presented to you. You are told what a great idea it would be for you to "buy" this right now. Sounds logical. Sounds good. Sounds like a "good buy." Yet no matter how much you try to shake it off, you feel a Thummim.

Unfortunately that "lust of the eyes" wins over and you make your investment. I do not need to tell you the ending to this story, because you already know, only too well, how it ends! Guess what? You did not listen to the Lord! He was talking to you!

On the other side of the coin, (this is where I live) the Lord might prompt you to buy something or invest your finances into something that does not make sense. You feel a peace in your spirit about it, but then those annoying thoughts start to creep in.

"This is the last of our money, what if nothing else comes in?"

"Do we *really* need this right now? Aren't I just being frivolous?"

"Why should I get two, when one will do?"

"I think we need to watch every dollar we have. I need to shop around and see if it is cheaper somewhere else."

Yes I know – pretty naturalistic huh? The crazy thing is, you bring your needs before the Lord all the time. You ask Him for direction regarding your finances. You pray for Him to provide your need. Then when He tells you to use what you have, in a certain direction, you question Him!

I am reminded of the widow who invested the last little bit of flour and oil that she had, into feeding Elijah. Do you think that her investment was a waste of time? Being frivolous with what she had, fed her, Elijah and her son for the duration of the famine!

Think back on the last week. How many times have you fought the promptings of the Holy Spirit, in every area of your life? Have I challenged you enough yet? Good! Now the next time you feel that Urim or Thummim, do not say to yourself, "Oh yes, that is a good suggestion, I will decide if I want to obey or not… "

Rather say, "Lord Jesus, not my will, but yours be done!"

This is just the first simple way that God can give you His rhema word. Now go out and apply it with the faith He gives it with. You can only experience success from here on out!

CHAPTER 04

PROPHETIC DREAMS: EXPLORING THEIR PURPOSE

Chapter 04 – Prophetic Dreams: Exploring Their Purpose

> *Job 33*
> *15 In a dream, in a vision of the night, when deep sleep falls upon men, while slumbering on their beds;*

Next to journaling, dreams are one of the ways the Lord speaks to me the most. This is true for most prophets. In fact, it is through these dreams that you start to feel drawn to the realm of the prophetic in the first place.

Understanding the Parables

The Word is full of types and shadows. The Lord Jesus Himself spoke in parables. However, we find something interesting when we see Him explaining the parable of the sower to His disciples. Notice what He says here:

> *Luke 8*
> *9 Then His disciples asked Him, saying, "What does this parable mean?"*
> *10 And He said, "To you it has been given to know the mysteries of the kingdom of God, but to the rest it is given in parables, that 'Seeing they may not see, and hearing they may not understand.'*

In my original book I emphasized the concept of parables, which still remain the main aspect of dream interpretation. Yet in the passage above Jesus says something interesting to His disciples. He says that to them is made known the mysteries of the kingdom of God, but to others in parables!

In other words, because the disciples had a closer relationship with Jesus, He spoke to them differently. What the others saw it types and shadows, they got to see clearly.

GETTING THE CONCEPT

So to clarify - your dreams are like parables. The Lord is telling you a story to get His message across to you. In the same way that Jesus' parables had deeper meanings, so do your dreams. Now, had Jesus told everyone the parable of the Good Samaritan, it would have been odd for someone in the crowd to rush out and try to find the real man Jesus was talking about.

No, the parable was clear – Jesus was telling a story; using pictures they could relate to, to get a message across to them. The same holds true to your dreams. The Lord is using pictures that are common to you and to the Word, to give you a message.

Now, how the Lord tells that story is going to evolve as you rise up into prophetic office. There will be times whene He will speak to you as He did to Daniel, and other times when He will speak to you as He did to Paul!

Daniel was shown visions that were so deep with imagery and intention that even today, scholars are still digging gold from them! Then on the other hand, you have the Lord speaking to Paul in a night vision and telling him clearly, "Stay in this city!" There was no hidden meaning there!

The point is, as a prophet you should be sensitive to hearing God through your dreams in both ways. Learn to identify and interpret the symbols. Then also be sensitive to know when the Lord is "talking to you straight."

THREE MAIN PROPHETIC DREAM GROUPS

1. Internal (Personal) Prophetic Dream
2. External Prophetic Dream for the Church
3. External Prophetic Dream for Others

I am mentioning these groups here now, but will discuss them at greater length in Chapter 7. I want to take your hand and help you navigate through the many dreams that you have and help you find their place. Like I said, you already know how to categorize your dreams, so this is all about applying them. If you do not already know the steps to interpreting your dream, read *The Way of Dreams and Visions*.

In the next chapter I will give you a quick explanation on dream types if you need to "brush up" on the various categories of dreams that we have.

APPLYING THE REVELATION

Let me drill my point home again – a rhema word is no good unless it is applied!

For way too long now, prophets have used dreams much like psychics use soothsaying.

There is a purpose for your dreams! The Lord is giving you these revelations to call you to action. They are not just for the purpose of looking good. They are not so that you can tell everyone about your great spiritual experiences.

You are having these "great" spiritual experiences so that you can act on them in faith! We miss this badly sometimes as prophets. We get so excited about what the Lord is saying, that we forget to follow up that revelation with obedience.

PROPHETIC DREAMS: EXPLORING THEIR PURPOSE

1. FOR THE PURPOSE OF INSTRUCTION

> *Jeremiah 23*
> *28 "The prophet who has a dream, let him tell a dream; And he who has My word, let him speak My word faithfully. What is the chaff to the wheat?" says the Lord.*

> *Daniel 7*
> *1 In the first year of Belshazzar king of Babylon, Daniel had a dream and visions of his head while on his bed. Then he wrote down the dream, telling the main facts.*

Joseph sure got the concept of this principle! Of course the dreams he shared got him into a heap of trouble. No one wants to hear that their little brother will become "Mr. High and Mighty" and that they will need to bow down to him!

Yet it was the declaration of these dreams, that reminded his brothers of God's will when the time came. Very often the Lord will give you a prophetic dream for the purpose of instruction.

TEACHERS DREAM TOO

It will not surprise you then to hear that even teachers can have a dream like this! This is a dream that will give you a principle. In the passage above, Daniel wrote down the "visions of the night" that he received and so we have many fascinating chapters in the book of Daniel.

As I have come to the Lord to teach on a specific subject, it is not uncommon for me to dream about it! As I seek the Lord about what to teach and how to go about my message, He will give me a dream that will put the missing pieces in place.

Keep in mind that He will always use symbols that are familiar to you. He will speak in types and in shadows. However, you should already be at the place where you can identify those symbols, so I will not labor that point.

The point I do want to make though, is that if you have sought the Lord for a principle or an answer to a specific problem, it is common for Him to answer that problem with a dream of instruction!

Personal Example: Instructional Prophetic Dream

This kind of prophetic dream is one that you can share with others. I had such a dream when writing the *Practical Prophetic Ministry* book. The Lord gave me a dream of going on a journey where I was pregnant and after having the baby, I went to find others who were pregnant and to be their midwife. He showed me how this was one of the roles of the prophet.

I share the full dream in the actual book, so that other prophets can be encouraged by it. So many have read it and shared how they received a similar revelation from the Lord. There are times to write your dreams down, but please only do so when they contain a principle.

So to put it in a nutshell for you – If the Lord gives you a dream for the purpose of instruction, it will contain a principle that can be retaught many times.

Key Principle

> An instructional prophetic dream will line up with the Word and will resonate with others who are on this particular spiritual walk.

By all means, write such a dream down and share it to instruct others. Do not, however, write down all your prophetic dreams in the hope of bringing inspiration –

the Church lacks power at times, but there is most certainly no lack right now for "prophets" with astounding revelations, that they have the desperate need to share!

2. FOR THE PURPOSE OF DIRECTION

> *Acts 18*
> *9 Now the Lord spoke to Paul in the night by a vision, Do not be afraid, but speak, and do not keep silent:*

Often a dream will be for the purpose of direction. Its intent is to tell you which step to take next in your walk with God. The Lord often spoke to people in Scripture to tell them what to do.

If you read this account in the books of Acts, you will see that Paul stayed for a full year and a half in this region before moving on. This was a bit out of the norm for him, because his usual modus operandi was the "evangelize and run" kind of itinerary.

We understand that the reason for this, was because he had a habit of making the Pharisees jealous and the pagans manifest and so he had to run for his life very often. (Ah yes people... that scenario is still alive and well in the Church today, isn't it?)

However, back to my point... Joseph and Mary are a great example of the Lord sending an angel, in a dream, to tell them when to leave Egypt.

Another example of this, is when Paul dreamt of the Macedonian beckoning him to come to them. If you have had your eyes focused on a goal that the Lord has given to you, then to receiving a dream giving you the "next step", is right in line!

PERSONAL EXAMPLE: DIRECTIONAL PROPHETIC DREAM

When I came to writing this book, there were some things I was not sure of. I was asking the Lord for direction on the focus for this book. It did not take long and the Lord gave me the strangest dream!

I dreamed that I was in a bathroom (which speaks of a cleansing process) and in front of me lay a baby girl. In the dream I had given birth to her years before, but had given her away.

I did not feel bad about giving her away. Somehow in the dream I felt like this was exactly what I was meant to do. In the middle of this though, people started putting pressure on me. They said that I was being a bad person to let it go! I should take her and raise her and be responsible! In the dream I felt the obligation and struggle.

When I woke up and shared the dream with my team, the Lord began speaking to me so clearly. You see I could identify those symbols in my dream and I knew very well that the baby girl spoke of a prophetic anointing I had in the past. One that the Lord had asked me to give up, so that I could move on to teaching about the prophetic and not just operating in it.

I knew exactly what God was saying. There were some things I was feeling "obligated" to put into this book because of what I had been taught in the past. The Lord reassured me, "Let it go! I want you to write something fresh. Do not feel compelled to dig up the things of the past."

This was just the direction I needed and the pages that you hold in your hands are the fruit of that.

3. FOR THE PURPOSE OF WARNING

What of the warning dream? Right through Scripture you read of where the Lord spoke a warning.

> *Genesis 20*
> *3 But God came to Abimelech in a dream by night, and said to him, Indeed you are a dead man because of the woman whom you have taken, for she is a man's wife.*

KEY PRINCIPLE

> A warning dream is always directional. It will tell you what to look out for and what to do about it.

When the Lord gives you a warning of what the enemy would like to do in your life, this is not for the purpose of causing fear. Instead, you are meant to use the authority and means He has given you, to overcome that evil plan.

This warning is not just restricted to the work of the enemy, just like this dream depicts. When we think of the term "warning dream" we immediately link it to "attack from the enemy." However, in my experience the greatest damage we can experience is the damage we do to ourselves!

Many of the warning dreams the Lord will give you, will warn against your own flesh. It will warn you against a direction that is not of Him. He will give you such a dream to warn you of a snare that the enemy has put on your road ahead.

So a warning dream can be one of two things. It can warn you of a work of the enemy. Secondly, it can be a warning concerning your own flesh and the direction you are taking.

Personal Example: Warning Prophetic Dream

Excuse my flesh as I get personal here. There is no better way to show you what I mean, than to point to my own flesh in this example.

The Lord has often used warning dreams to caution me against a wrong direction. There are a couple of symbols that He uses, but there is one in particular that always makes me wake up and start repenting!

If I dream that I have broken or rotten teeth, I know God is trying to warn me. Ok, don't laugh! I will never forget the first time I started having these dreams.

I was still in the throes of prophetic training and not sure what they meant at first. So I began to look into the Word. The more I looked into it, the more I saw how broken teeth and soft bones were the Lord's way of saying, "Something is eating you up from the inside!"

As I brought the dream to Him, He told me so plainly, "I am trying to show you that you have bitterness raging inside of you! This bitterness is stealing your strength and the goodness I have given to you. This bitterness is making you weak and leading you astray."

I quickly came to understand what the passage meant that says, "Lay aside every weight that easily besets you… "

The Lord was warning me of impending doom! If I did not let go of the bitterness that was eating me up on the inside, I was headed for disaster. I am glad to say that these dreams are not as frequent like they were in the early days. However, even today, if I have such a dream, the message is clear.

I wake up repenting! I think back on the day before, and sure enough, a conflict "got under my skin" and I responded incorrectly. Thank the Lord for this kind of warning!

If the Lord has been warning you in this same way, grab hold of it! This kind of warning is the rudder in your spiritual ship. It will make sure that you steer your boat in the right direction and won't end up shipwrecking your faith.

4. FOR THE PURPOSE OF CONFIRMATION

More than once you may have had a dream that has confirmed a direction that God has already given to you.

When you receive a vision or a prophetic word from the Lord, you might feel uncertain if you heard Him. The Lord will often give you a dream to confirm that you are on the right track.

I love the use of this purpose in the following passage:

> *Matthew 2*
> *22 But when he heard that Archelaus was reigning over Judea instead of his father Herod, he was afraid to go there. And being warned by God in a dream, he turned aside into the region of Galilee:*

Joseph was already afraid of going back to Judea and was already feeling that they had to take a different route. This dream confirmed his fears and gave him the direction he needed.

Personal Experience

There are times as a leader when I feel God leading us in a new direction, but feel uncertain of my revelation. This is especially true when it comes to some risky moves!

When you have others following you and your decision can change their lives, you can be sure that you take that step with its fair share of fear and trembling.

In these moments, the Lord has never let me down. Either He will give me a word of confirmation through another prophet, or He will give me a dream. I have had this more times than I can count.

For the longest time our main ministry was involved in Europe. The Lord started shifting our attention, and Craig and I felt that we needed to focus more on the United States.

It was a big step that carried some risks. I asked the Lord for more confirmation and it came that evening in the form of a dream.

I dreamed that I met the president of the United States and his wife. He welcomed me into his home and as I entered, I moved around and started helping them with decisions and was involved in their lives.

The dream was clear. The president and his wife were a picture of the American people and the Lord's confirmation was clear, "I am sending you to my church in America!"

Do you see once again how important it is to interpret the symbols in your dream correctly? To add to your already growing knowledge on the subject, I will talk in a later chapter on specific symbols that are likely common to you.

5. For the Purpose of Motivation

Is it so hard to believe that the Lord would give you a dream just for the joy of it? I cannot count the number of times, I was in the Lord's presence and He told me things simply to lift my spirit.

> *Psalms 16*
> *11 You will show me the path of life; in Your presence is fullness of joy; it Your right hand are pleasures forevermore.*

There is a reason that David ran into the presence of the Lord so often! It was there that He found his joy and peace. As a prophet, coming to receive encouragement during your times of prayer, should be normal.

Well then, why not receive them through dreams? I think that sometimes we get too "deep" and try to interpret everything way too quickly. Sometimes the Lord just wants to encourage you to keep going on.

You will have dreams that have a single purpose – to motivate you!

Consider this passage:

Genesis 28
12 Then he dreamed, and behold, a ladder was set up on the earth, and its top reached to heaven; and there the angels of God were ascending and descending on it.

We all know this account in Scripture. It was through this vision that the Lord gave Jacob the motivation he needed. It was in this moment that He revealed Himself to Jacob. Can you imagine how Jacob felt at the moment of having this dream?

He had just kissed his mother and father goodbye, with his brother breathing death threats. He was young and alone, heading to a place he had never seen before. He did not know what awaited him. He was alone and uncertain.

It is in moments like these that the Lord will reach out and motivate you. He will say, "I am here! I am going to see you through this. I am going to bless you."

Personal Experience

So if you have a dream that encourages you, but does not seem to have a message for the future, then rest in what God is saying.

I had a dream once where I was going through a difficult time. The Lord felt so far away and I certainly needed a spiritual lift.

That night I dreamed that I was a beautiful bride. I had long hair, and a lovely ring on my finger. In the dream I felt loved and excited for the future.

I woke up feeling on top of the world. The Lord was just confirming to me, "My child I love you. You are my bride and you are precious to me."

KEY PRINCIPLE

> Sometimes we do not need to dig for deeper meanings. Sometimes we just need to take our dreams as they are, and enjoy the moment of encouragement they were meant to be.

Out of all 5 purposes I have listed here, 4 of them need to be applied. The dreams that encourage and motivate you, are simply there for you to be filled up with the spirit of the Lord.

The others call on you for action; to heed the warning, follow the instruction and press through with the confirmation. Dreams are rightly called "night visions" for just as you need to apply any revelation you get in prayer, so also should you apply it when receiving them through dreams.

Chapter 05

The Skinny of Dream Categories

Chapter 05 – The Skinny of Dream Categories

Before you can begin to understand what the characters in your dreams represent, it is a good idea to categorize them first.

This chapter is a brief summary of what I cover in *The Way of Dreams and Visions*. So if you do not have that book, you can still get some basics, to help you through the next couple of chapters.

You need to identify if your dream is a healing, internal, prophetic or prophetic dream, or if it is just a collection of rubbish that you fed into your mind that day.

Once you have identified the dream as internal or prophetic, write it down and move on to step 2.

Here are some hints on how to identify which category the dream falls into.

A. Prophetic

> *Key Principle*
>
> The most outstanding aspect of a prophetic dream is that you are not a participant. In dreams like this, you will find yourself standing on the outside and watching the events.

As a prophet, this category comes to life for you! In Chapter 7 I will delve deeper into how the Lord speaks to prophets in dreams, but before deciding that your dream is prophetic, familiarize yourself with the other dream categories first.

A prophetic dream is very clear. It is a short, clear dream with a single message. Often you will have a few short dreams one after the other, each having a similar message.

This dream category concerns future events. It functions like the word of wisdom and needs to be used with discernment. Daniel is a prime example with the external prophetic dreams he received, with regards to Israel and the empires of his time. His dreams always had a future orientation.

Joseph also interpreted the external dream of the King of Egypt, which allowed him to save many lives, even the lives of his nation. Note how even external dreams are given in symbolism. Even in an external dream, the characters may not be who they are in real life.

B. Healing

In a healing dream, you will most likely relive past events. You may find yourself saying things in your dream you had wished you had said, in that particular circumstance.

In a healing dream, you will visit your past and walk through old houses, events or time frames in your life and re-experience an event, but this time with a happy ending.

This is also a dream where you seem to be running or hiding from something and then finally confronting what is chasing you. This particular scenario is very characteristic of a healing dream.

You might even wake up crying or laughing after a dream like this.

C. Garbage Dream

A dream that is over-complicated, with many events and scenery changes, is very likely just to be your inner man "throwing out" the junk it has accumulated during the day.

You will most likely have many garbage dreams if you get more into the Word and spend time with the Lord. This happens because your mind is making space for the Word and will "throw out" the garbage you have stored in there for years.

A dream, where you display emotions and characteristics that are not natural to you, are simply your sub-conscious "living out" those feelings and hidden temptations that you experienced during the day. These dreams are simply purging and do not have an interpretation.

D. INTERNAL AND INTERNAL PROPHETIC DREAMS

KEY PRINCIPLE

> The most outstanding aspect of an internal dream is that you are the "star of the show."

Next to garbage dreams, this dream type will be the most common you will experience.

They are a picture of what is going on in your spirit right now. As a prophet though, you will receive a lot of direction for the future in these dreams.

So, in identifying, if your dream falls under the "internal dreams" category, ask yourself, "Was I the main star?"

If this is the case, the dream is internal and the characters symbolic of something of yourself.

THE INTERNAL DREAM

An internal dream, will often give you direction for your spiritual life. It functions the same way, as a Word of knowledge, in that it relates to things of the past and present.

An internal dream always depicts the present condition of your spiritual life. It will let you know if you have gotten off the path, or if you need to be placing more emphasis on something else.

It may also tell you when you have birthed something new in the spirit, have come to a place of rest, or are being geared for a promotion.

THE INTERNAL PROPHETIC DREAM

An internal prophetic dream has a slightly different emphasis. Joseph was a good example of this when the Lord gave him the dreams of his brothers' sheaves bowing to his sheaf, indicating that his family would one day, bow before him.

These dreams were internal because they concerned him personally, but yet they were also prophetic in that they were giving him a word for the future.

Another good example would be of the baker and butler whose dreams Joseph interpreted in prison. (Genesis 40:5) Both concerned them personally, but also gave a prophetic word of what was going to happen.

Internal prophetic dreams function the same as a word of wisdom - only the word pertains to you personally. The symbols in your dream represent a part of yourself.

DOUBLE INTERPRETATIONS

KEY PRINCIPLE

> It is entirely possible for a dream to have a personal and prophetic interpretation.

In looking at Nebuchadnezzar once again and his dream of the large statue, we hear only the external interpretation that Daniel gave the King.

Daniel told the King how an empire was going to come that would live forever (speaking of the Kingdom of God). What Daniel was too afraid to tell the King was that Nebuchadnezzar himself, was going to be toppled and destroyed. He left out the part later in the dream where the tree that was felled and made to be a stump in the dew for 7 years. Here the Lord revealed what would happen to Nebuchadnezzar personally.

So while the Lord may give you an internal dream pertaining to your spiritual condition, He may also give you a prophetic dream relating to the future.

I have often seen many people err in classifying all their dreams as external, overlooking the internal interpretation.

Perhaps this is because people do not like to have such a close look at themselves, and would rather relate the atrocities and obvious mistakes revealed in their dreams as pertaining to the Church or a nation.

Prophetic Dreams – Why and When

When you first begin to come into a relationship with the Lord Jesus, it takes you a while to realize that He wants to converse with you.

Before you get to know His nature, you cannot help but feel that He talks when He wants and ignores you when He wants to. And so we, like everyone else with a hunger to know Him, begin by just hoping and praying that He will talk.

The closer you walk with Jesus and the more you study the Word though, this thinking begins to change. You come to realize that Jesus is talking all the time!

You come to realize that He wants to have ongoing fellowship with you. Through the process of journaling you have a "back and forth." When you start journaling you quickly learn that the Lord talks in line with what you ask. He is a gentleman. He cares about what you have to say and He cares about touching on the things that really matter to you.

You come to learn that He answers the questions you ask! When you pray, He gives you visions according to what you are praying for.

Just like when Daniel asked the Lord about the dream of the King, so also does God hear your prayer! When Daniel came to the Lord and sought Him regarding the King's dream, the Lord answered. Not only did He give the same dream to Daniel, but He also supplied the interpretation!

Key Principle

> And so, just like the Lord answers what you are praying for with visions and confirmation, so will He also use dreams to answer your prayer.

Dreams Do Not "Come out of Nowhere"

In other words, if you were seeking the Lord about something before you went to bed, what you dream that night will be the revelation you were seeking.

We often overlook this powerful principle. You have a dream and think to yourself, "Where did that come from?" Well, let me tell you where it came from!

It came from your faith! That dream came as an answer to the cry of your heart.

THE MISSING STEP

I have taught up until now to determine the category of your dream and also to break down the symbols. However, there is a missing step!

This step is to ask these questions:

"What was I praying for before going to bed?"

"What is continually on my heart and mind at the moment?"

"What was I reading or contemplating before going to bed or over the last few days?"

What you might not realize is that the Lord has been trying to intervene in your circumstances! Unfortunately, if you do not connect your dream to what you have been praying about, you could miss the answer you have been seeking Him for.

The Holy Spirit manifests the gifts of the Spirit as He wills. He could give you revelation through the Word, a vision or in this situation... through a dream! So before trying to determine what all the symbols in your dream mean, stop and take stock of what has been on your heart lately.

For example, if you have been praying a lot for your church, it would not be surprising for you to have a prophetic dream that will shed some light on what is going on in the Spirit.

FACING BEELZEBUB

I had an experience with this that clarifies my point pretty well. It happened as the Lord was teaching me more on spiritual warfare.

For some reason, during this time in my life I kept coming into confrontation with people bound with the New Age cult. Of course I could never have known how much this season equipped me, for facing believers still in bondage to this demonic stronghold, later in my ministry.

I was young and it was my first experience with people heavily involved in the New Age. I remember one particular situation. We had bumped into a group of them at a restaurant.

Out of nowhere one of the group eating at the table next to us felt "led" to walk over and just strike up conversation and to try and convince us that the angels they worshipped and the God we served were one and the same. That it was "all the same spirit." Needless to say – we did not have the same opinion!

That evening I had a dream. I dreamed that I confronted an awful looking demon. Instinctively I just knew that this was Beelzebub as spoken of in Scripture.

In my dream, I was standing in front of him, looking on. I saw how he had kingdoms under him and also how he controlled them. I felt his spirit. It was vulgar. I was not active in the dream, but saw how he controlled slaves under him, keeping them in bondage.

I woke up, not sure why I had that dream. One thing I never forgot was what I felt in that dream. If there is anyone with a New Age background or still bound by that demon, you can be sure I can sense that spirit from a mile away.

Why did I have this dream? I did not understand that for years. Looking back now it makes sense. It was what I was living at the time. It was the particular training that the Lord was taking me through. It was a building block for the future that my ministry would be established on.

For this season in my life, I had many such dreams. A time came though when the Lord led me in yet another direction. This time it was into a more intimate relationship with Jesus.

My dreams changed. I did not confront demons in my sleep any longer. Instead I started dreaming about being taken to a quiet place, or being dressed up as a bride. These dreams confirmed and expounded on what God was teaching me from day to day.

A Dream Shift

So if you had a certain kind of dream and then it stopped, do not be discouraged! What are you going through in your natural and spiritual life right now?

You have simply grown up and moved onto another season of spiritual growth.

Key Principle

> The Lord will give you dreams that will answer the cry of your heart in the present.

That is why even healing dreams happen after you have gone through a present day process of healing. When you dream of your past, you can be sure it is that your past problem is cropping up in your present.

Keep this principle in mind, and before rushing off to interpret your prophetic dream, determine what you have been praying about.

This is especially appropriate for prophetic dreams, because they will be an answer to what you interceded on behalf of others. I will talk more of this in Chapter 7. For now, I am going to break down a couple of common symbols found in your dreams. So pick up a pen and paper before moving on to the next chapter, because we are about to get even more practical!

CHAPTER 06

CHARACTER SPECIFIC AND UNIVERSAL SYMBOLS

Chapter 06 – Character Specific and Universal Symbols

There are so many symbols to interpret that it would take another hundred books to list them all. Instead what I am going to do in this chapter, is pick out ten of the most popular symbols that I come across all of the time.

These symbols are ones that I find coming up in my own dreams or in the dreams of others I minister to.

Jesus used parables to illustrate spiritual principles to the people of His day. He used pictures that were common to them. In the same way the Lord will still use symbols in our dreams that are common to us. The Lord still speaks to us in parables, even in our dreams.

These symbols are also ones that span across cultures and denominations. So by arming yourself with some good knowledge here, you will also start picking up the wisdom you need to minister effectively.

It is good to know that each of these symbols can have double meanings, just like I shared in the previous chapter. They can have an internal and a prophetic interpretation, depending on their context.

The Character Specific Symbol

There are symbols in your dream that are specific to you. These are symbols such as your pet cat "Fluffy", your mother, father and eldest child.

Dream Interpretation: Steps 2 and 3

These symbols have a specific meaning to you and will change for someone else. This is true even in a family. In your dreams, your father could speak of the Lord, while for your sister, he could speak of the flesh – it all really depends on your relationship with your father.

An internal dream is full of character specific symbols. It might interest you to know that you can even have "internal visions." In other words, visions that are specific just to you.

KEY PRINCIPLE

> A character specific symbol can only be applied to you, because the interpretation is based on your personal convictions and not on those of the Word.

The interpretation of these symbols change depending on your gender, culture, upbringing and personal emotions.

THE UNIVERSAL SYMBOL

In contrast, universal symbols can be applied to every believer, because these can be found in the Word.

> **KEY PRINCIPLE**
> Universal dream and vision symbols can be applied to every gender, culture and denomination, because their source is the Word of God. The Word never changes.

It might interest you to know that many of them have the same meaning even in visions. For now, determine what they mean to you and also make a note of what their universal meaning is (based on the Word).

1. GIVING BIRTH OR BEING PREGNANT

Isaiah 8
3 Then I went to the prophetess, and she conceived and bore a son. Then the Lord said to me, "Call his name Maher- Shalal- Hash- Baz;
4 for before the child shall have knowledge to cry "My father' and 'My mother,' the riches of Damascus and the spoil of Samaria will be taken away before the king of Assyria.

A baby symbolizes the birth of something new. This is not always a positive thing. It can be negative as well. Not all of the things that we conceive in our lives are good.

Dream Interpretation: Steps 2 and 3

This is true of this passage in Isaiah, where the birth of his son was symbolic of the birth of evil, that was about to come upon the children of Israel.

And so, not everything that you conceive in the spirit is something that you want. It is important to discern if the pregnancy or the birth in your dream is positive.

If you dream of being pregnant, it means that you have conceived something. Say for example, you have been studying a prophetic or teaching course and you dream that you are pregnant. It is a confirmation from the Lord that something has been conceived in you.

The principles that you are learning have started to take root in your spirit. It is a lovely dream, telling you that your new ministry has been conceived and will be born.

Personal Example

I remember when I had been released into ministry training, and about three months into it, I had such a clear dream. I dreamed that I was three months pregnant. I did not realize at the time that I had been on that road three months already.

The Lord was confirming that I was exactly on the track that He wanted me to be on. It was a message to nurture this new ministry, and to continue pressing on with it.

That is an important aspect of this kind of dream. In the natural, an expecting mother cannot just eat what she wants to. In the spirit it is the same. If you dream of being pregnant, it is not only a confirmation that you have conceived something new in the spirit, but also a message to nurture and care for that new thing.

FOR THE MEN

Now as a man, you might not dream that you are pregnant. You could dream instead that your wife is pregnant, and it would have the same interpretation. Just like in our passage in Isaiah – his wife was the one to have the baby and not him. However, it was still a clear picture of something that was about to "spring forth."

Because your wife is one with you, if you dream she is pregnant or giving birth, it means that you are birthing something new.

Now, if you have been seeking the Lord on behalf of a ministry and you are standing on the outside and watching a birth take place, this speaks of something new that the Lord is about to do in that ministry.

MISCARRIAGE. LOSING THE BABY

Perhaps you dreamed that you lost the baby or that it was stillborn. This sounds like a terrible dream at first. However, think about it for a bit. Could it be that the thing that you conceived was not of God? If what you are "pregnant with" is a bad thing, then this dream would have a positive meaning.

Perhaps you were involved in a relationship in the past and you dream of being pregnant from that person. In your dream, your circumstances take you back to that time in your life. Your dream is indicating that you conceived something back in that time, that has now been brought to death.

While that might seem negative at first, it could well be that it is exactly what God wants to do in your life right now. Perhaps He is calling you to let an old vision die or to let go of an old responsibility.

Not everything we conceive in the spirit is positive. There are times we receive negative things. On the other hand, there are times when seasons pass and the Lord calls us to pick up new ministries and mandates, meaning you have to let the old go.

GIVING BIRTH/HOLDING A BABY

To dream of giving birth or of holding a baby, speaks of a new responsibility that you have been given. Again, this dream has a double meaning.

On the one hand, the Lord has given you a ministry or a calling and placed it into your hands, but on the other, your job has just begun! It is for you now to take hold of that calling and to do something with it.

I never saw a baby that was born and left to take care of itself. It is for you to work from there.

Breastfeeding

> Isaiah 60
> 16 You shall drink the milk of the Gentiles, and milk the breast of kings; you shall know that I, the Lord, am your Savior and your Redeemer, the Mighty One of Jacob.

Breastfeeding has a double meaning depending on its context. It can either speak of nurturing something, or in the case of this passage, it means that something is feeding you!

This passage in Isaiah says that you will "suck the breast of kings." In other words, it means that you will be given the best of those who "have it all." This speaks of favor and of receiving the goodness from this world.

Key Principle

> Breastfeeding a baby in your dream speaks of investing everything you are and all of your strengths, into this new spiritual baby.

When it speaks of your ministry, this is a fantastic picture.

It means that the Lord is confirming that now is the time to put your full effort into this ministry. He is encouraging you to put everything into this one thing instead of running around, wasting your time on other things that do not matter.

If you are breastfeeding someone else's baby though, you need to determine if you are pouring out all your resources correctly or if you are giving something out that you should be putting towards your "own baby."

For example, if you have been praying about serving in a ministry and you dream of breastfeeding a baby (in a positive context), it could well mean that the Lord is telling you to invest the goodness you have, into this ministry and to not hold back.

GIVING A BABY AWAY. OTHER PEOPLE'S BABIES

You can have dreams where you give your baby away. This is a confirmation that the ministry you are working with, is something that the Lord wants you to hand over to someone else.

The Lord wants you to hand the care of that ministry over to someone else, so that He can give you something new.

At first, this might seem negative, but if you understand the symbol, it is quite positive. This is not easy of course. The ministry has become your baby and you have put your heart and soul into it and it is not easy to pass it on. However, until you are prepared to do this, you will not receive the new baby that the Lord has for you.

Now there is also a negative side. What if you keep dreaming that you are caring for other people's babies, or that you keep being handed other people's babies?

Do you know the English expression, "That's not my baby!"

Why do you think we say that? It speaks of our responsibilities and cares. So if you keep being dumped with other people's babies in your dreams, it means that other people keep dumping their junk on you.

They are putting their responsibility on you and instead of investing your time into the ministry God has given you, you are running around investing into the ministries of others. This is a negative dream.

The Lord is trying to say, "You are so busy running around fussing over everyone else and putting so many fires out, that you are not taking care of the ministries and gifts that I have given to you."

People do not like to hear that interpretation very much. They like to hear that they are a nice person who just runs around helping others with their ministries. However, it is one thing to be a foster parent - it is another to give birth to your child. Even as a father, you want your own child.

You do not want to always give back the babies you care for. Instead you want to have your own child and see it grow up.

There is an exception however. You might dream that someone gives you their baby for a season to take care of. Then when that season is over, you hand the baby back. In this case, the Lord is indicating that there is some task that you are going to do, but it is not permanent. You will be there to help these people get off the ground, but you will not stay.

Remember, it is their baby – it is not your baby. This season is temporary.

2. DEATH

> *Romans 6*
> *8 Now if we died with Christ, we believe that we shall also live with Him,*

> *Romans 8*
> *13 For if you live according to the flesh you will die; but if by the Spirit you put to death the deeds of the body, you will live.*

A dream about death can feel very contradictory. You would think that dreaming of someone dying or of death would mean something terrible is in store, but the opposite is often true.

> **KEY PRINCIPLE**
>
> To dream of death often means that the Lord is bringing an aspect of your flesh to death, so that you can resurrect with something new.

Now what about a dream where a person keeps trying to get out of the coffin and will not die? What a horrible dream! Do you know what it means? It means that whatever aspect of yourself that the Lord is trying to crucify in you, keeps coming back to life.

MINISTRY TRAINING – DIE ALREADY!

You refuse to die and let go! It is time for you to bury that nasty flesh so that the Lord can be glorified in you. This kind of dream or vision is common to someone going through intense fivefold ministry training.

If you keep dreaming that someone keeps sitting up in a coffin, the Lord is saying to you, "Die already!"

And you respond with, "But Lord I did die! I let it all go."

"If you died, then you would not flinch! A dead body does not sit up!"

When Jesus died, He truly died. He only rose up when the Father revived Him. If you are in prophetic training or office, get ready for this! The Lord will call you to death again and again so that you can become more effective for Him.

Each time that you rise up in your flesh or try to do things your way, you can bet that a good "death experience" is on the way.

PEOPLE YOU KNOW OR BABIES DYING

Perhaps you dreamed of a close family member dying. The first thing you need to identify is what that person means to you in real life. That will give you a good indication of what the Lord is trying to bring to death in you.

This is something to keep in mind when you are interpreting for others. You need to ask them what that person means to them in real life.

Now, what happens if you dream one of your babies dies? The Lord is saying, "I am taking you through a death of a vision."

If the dream is negative, then one of your ministries or something you are involved with is under attack at the moment and the enemy is trying to destroy it.

3. CRYING IN YOUR SLEEP

Most people have done it. I have even been known to giggle in my sleep from time to time. (No... you are not the only one!) So what is that all about? Rest assured that this is nothing to worry about. This is simply a purging dream.

It means that all the tension that you have built up is being released. Perhaps you dreamed of something from your past and that caused the crying. This could mean that the Lord is bringing a healing to that area in your life. On the other hand, it could mean that He is exposing an area in your life that still needs healing.

If you suspect that there is an emotional wound that the Lord is exposing, do not be afraid. The Lord is exposing it only to heal it. He is not exposing it to hurt you.

4. YOUR HOUSE

> *1 Samuel 2*
> *35 Then I will raise up for Myself a faithful priest who shall do according to what is in My heart and in My mind. I will build him a sure house, and he shall walk before My anointed forever.*

This symbol is as common as the one on babies! I love this passage because it speaks of an eternal house for the Lord. It is speaking of you and me! We are the house that He now lives in!

And so it is good to remember that the house you dream about, speaks of your life. Now it is not often that you will dream of the actual house you are living in right now.

In your dreams, the house might look different to what you have now, but in the dream it is your house. You might even dream of houses you grew up in or have certain memories of. In each case the house belongs to you and so represents an aspect of your life.

We are the temple of the Holy Spirit and dreaming of a house is a picture of what is happening in you right now.

NEW ROOMS

Say for example that you dream you suddenly discover new rooms in your house. When I first started moving more into the arts, I kept having a dream like that. I kept dreaming of finding new rooms in my house. At first I could not understand what it meant, but then I realized that there were some untapped areas in my life that I had never tried going into before.

However, now was the time to tap into that hidden potential. After I received the interpretation, I did not have the dreams any more. The interpretation was clear. I had to go into areas that I always had, but had never developed.

A HOUSE BEING TORN DOWN OR RENOVATED

Of course there was the time I dreamed my entire house was being torn down! Bad dream! Do you know what that means? It means that the Lord is about to do some renovating in your life. And you know, it is not a lot of fun to have a wall knocked down. It is not comfortable at all.

So if you dream something like that, then get ready for some shaking in your life. The Lord is about to change your foundation and give you a face-lift. If you are in ministry, then deal with it! Your house is going to be changed more often than you can count.

When someone comes to you for an interpretation of dreams involving their house, you now have an answer for them. It all depends on what is happening in the house. If the house is being expanded, it means that the Lord is going to expand them.

Just by knowing that the house represents your life, the interpretation opens up immediately.

5. Relatives

I have given such a lengthy description of this one in the *Dreams and Visions Symbol Dictionary*, but let me just say that you will dream of relatives and close friends very often.

Now is the time to be honest and consider what you really think of that person. And so the easiest way to assess what a relative means in your dream is to do this:

1. Close your eyes and say their name.

2. What is the first word that comes to your mind?

3. What was going on in your life when this person appeared on the scene (especially appropriate for the birth of your children)

What is the first image or impression that comes to your mind? How about we apply this now and play a little game together?

I am going to write down a list of a few people that should be fairly common in your life. After you read each one on the list, close your eyes, say their name and then write down the first word or impression that comes to you.

If nothing comes to your mind as you go through the list, do not worry! It could be that they are not a common symbol in your life. This is just a practice round and one that you can use with others as you minister.

Here it goes!

1. Mother

2. Father

3. Mother-In-Law

4. Father-In-Law

5. Eldest Sister (siblings)

6. Your Eldest Child (If you have children)

7. Husband/Wife

When I dream of my husband, I know the Lord is speaking of my relationship with Jesus. When I dream of my relationship with my husband, I know that Jesus is pointing out areas that I need to work on, or perhaps good things that He is doing.

My Father though is a picture of God the Father in my dreams and these dreams speak of my direction for ministry. Just as our heavenly Father opens doors for us or closes them.

When I dream of my stepmother I know the Lord is talking to me of the Church and His love for her. My eldest child has always been a picture of my faith, while each of my spiritual children represent various aspects of my ministry.

It is pretty common though for your father to speak of the Lord in your dream. It is no surprise considering that he was the first picture you ever had of authority and of the Lord.

For many, their first child speaks of their ministry, because the child is a picture of something new that was born. For me, each of my children represent something different. I was pregnant with Rebekah when I was placed in apostolic office. Since that time, every time I dream of her, I know that the Lord is speaking to me about my apostolic call.

Determine what your relationship is like with each person and the picture will quickly fall into place.

STRUGGLING WITH INTIMACY

If you dream that you keep trying to get intimate with your spouse but you are struggling, it could indicate a personal spiritual struggle that you are having, to get into an intimate relationship with the Lord. The Lord is trying to let you know that there are so many distractions in your life right now that you are struggling to come closer.

There are just too many voices and responsibilities that keep pulling you in so many directions, that your very relationship with the Lord is starting to suffer.

You need to learn to be honest and real with yourself. Dreams are there to give you direction, and sure, when you are interpreting for others, now is not the time to expose all your shortcomings.

When you are ministering, it is the time to come across with confidence, so that the person you are ministering to can have faith in you. However, when it comes to dealing with personal dreams and struggles, be honest with yourself and face your flesh, so that the Lord can give you what you need to overcome it.

6. DREAMING OF FLYING

> *Psalms 55*
> *6 So I said, "Oh, that I had wings like a dove! I would fly away and be at rest.*
> *7 Indeed, I would wander far off, and remain in the wilderness.*

When I looked at this symbol when I did the *Symbol Dictionary*, He gave me such a clear picture. King David shares in Psalm 55, saying that if only he could be a dove, that he would fly to the wilderness. When I read that scripture, suddenly all my "flying dreams" made sense.

If you dream of flying or trying to fly, it means that you are trying to escape. You are trying to escape the problems and pressures that you are facing right now. You need to determine if this is positive or not.

Flying With Freedom

Perhaps you are flying high above the mountains and valleys and you are soaring in the clouds. In the dream you feel free and full of joy. This is a wonderful picture of how it is in the realm of the spirit. The Word says that we are seated in heavenly places with the Lord.

The Lord is saying that you can fly high above your problems. This speaks of walking in freedom, high above your cares. You can see things from His perspective and you do not need to become bogged down with the cares of this life. After these dreams, you wake up feeling fantastic.

The Lord is telling you to look at things from His perspective. You can escape the problems of life if you run into His arms. He is far above the problems you are having, and with Him you can soar like an eagle.

CANNOT GET OFF THE GROUND

On the other hand, you might have a dream where you keep trying to fly, but you cannot seem to get off the ground. You are running and jumping and trying to fly, but you keep crashing down. This dream means that you are trying to escape the problems of life, but that they are overcoming you.

You need to discern if you are just trying to run away from your problems in life, because you do not want to face them, or if the problems are actually overwhelming you. I am more inclined to believe the former interpretation.

PEOPLE CHASING YOU

If you keep trying to jump, run, or fly away from people that are chasing you, the best thing that you can do in your dream is to stop and face those people.

It could be, that right now there are pressures in your life, that are coming on you and that you are trying to escape. You feel so stressed and overwhelmed with these cares and you just want to run away from them. However, the only way to overcome, is to stop and turn around and to deal with the pressures head-on. Only then can you soar like an eagle once again.

If you keep dreaming of trying to escape, then perhaps the Lord is telling you that it is time that you face your problems. You keep trying to find an easy way out, or a back door, but He is not going to give it to you. If you are ever going to overcome these pressures, it will mean facing them and working through them.

At the time that King David wrote about flying away, Absalom was chasing him and he had pressures all around him. Running away was not a solution. It was only when he stopped and faced his enemy that he overcame. David did not run away from Goliath, but he faced him.

Had David not faced and overcome all of the pressures that came on him as king, he would not have been the greatest one that ever lived.

You are not alone, if you feel like you want to run away from your problems. However, there are times you have to turn around to face those problems

7. HAIR

> *1 Corinthians 11*
> *14 Does not even nature itself teach you that if a man has long hair, it is a dishonor to him?*
> *15 But if a woman has long hair, it is a glory to her; for her hair is given to her for a covering.*

Perhaps this is a woman thing. We are always stressing about our hair. Before I preach or need to do a lecture on camera, the thing that takes me the longest is always my hair!

Hair is a very important part of a woman's image. This is not only relevant to our culture today, but it has been important since the time God created Eve. The

Scripture speaks of how the woman is the glory of the man, just as her hair is a glory to her.

It says that it is a shame for a woman to have a bald head, using it as an illustration for a woman without spiritual covering.

So when a woman dreams of her hair, the first thing it is speaking of is your image. When you change your hair, you change your whole appearance.

So when you dream of changes with your hair, the Lord is saying that He is taking you through a change of image.

He is saying that He is going to change who you are and change the way you view the world.

More importantly, hair is a picture of your covering. If you dreamed that your hair was being shaved, it would mean that you are not under the covering of your husband or your spiritual leader.

If you are a married woman, my first interpretation would mean that you are not under the covering of your husband.

The interpretation is the same if you dream your hair is falling out or being cut off. There is something wrong with your covering! Either you are not under cover, or there is something wrong with the covering you are under.

A Man With Long Hair

For a man, hair also speaks of their image. In fact, I know some men who are fussier about their hair than women are! So if you are a man and dream that you suddenly have long hair, this is not a good interpretation. In the New Testament, a man was discouraged from having long hair.

It could be that the Lord is saying that your image is perhaps too feminine. You need to change your image.

Going Bald (Men)

On the other hand, if your hair is falling out, it means that you are not under covering. However, if you have a fear of going bald in the natural, then losing your hair is a reflection of your inner fears.

8. Key

> Matthew 16
> 19 And I will give you the keys of the kingdom of heaven, and whatever you bind on earth will be bound in heaven, and whatever you loose on earth will be loosed in heaven.

When I give someone the key to my front door, I am giving them license and access to anything in my house. We had a tradition in South Africa where on your 21st birthday you got a big key. It is usually presented in a nice box and is a symbolic gift.

It is a picture of being given the "key to the house" In South Africa at 21 - you are officially regarded as an adult. So when you receive this key, it is an announcement that you are of age and now have the key and license to the house.

Just as a key speaks of authority in our culture, so does it speak of authority in the spirit as well.

I preach concerning the "prophetic key", but there are also other kinds of keys mentioned in scriptures.

When we see a brass key in the spirit, it often speaks of a teaching ministry. I have seen the apostolic key as a jewel encrusted key.

LOSING YOUR KEY

Now, what if you dream of losing your key, or of having it stolen? This is not good! It means that you are giving your license away. Now, if satan has your key it is not good. It means that he has been given license in your life and you need to take it back.

You have given him access to your life. It is time to close that door and rise up in your authority again. So whenever you see keys in the spirit or in your dreams, discern what kind of authority is being spoken about.

Across the board, it is speaking of authority and license. However, the kind of key it is, or the context of the dream will tell you exactly what kind of authority you are talking about.

Now, sometimes people dream of a key that looks like a fish. That sounds evangelistic to me. It speaks of an evangelistic authority. Use wisdom.

AT THE END OF THE DAY

I can tell you what the symbols mean and I can explain to you what I feel they are, but at the end of the day, it is for the Holy Spirit to give revelation and wisdom.

It is great to gather the knowledge in your head and you could study all of the symbols, but until you get wisdom and revelation to apply the interpretation, it means nothing.

So it is good that you are studying the principles, but once you have learned everything that you can and done everything that you can, it is time to put it all away.

Forget it all. Then flow out from your spirit and allow the Holy Spirit to direct you.

Take these explanations as an inspiration for what you have lived and seen in the Word for yourself.

A GOOD GUIDELINE TO FOLLOW

When a symbol from your dream can be traced to something directly from the Word, then it is a universal symbol that can be used for any culture or denomination.

If the symbol in your dream can only be found in your life, it relates to you and your present prayer burdens. So for example, if you dream of your father, the interpretation cannot be used in the life of another believer!

The dream relates to what you are going through right now. That symbol is yours personally. To dream of a key, giving birth or of a cross is different. These symbols come directly from the Word and they will mean the same for every believer.

These universal symbols will also have the same interpretation in visions. Learn to differentiate between the two, because you will need to have a full grasp of them, to understand the next chapter.

CHAPTER 07

3 Prophetic Dream Groups

Chapter 07 – 3 Prophetic Dream Groups

As a prophet there are three main groups that will be affected by your prophetic dreams. Of course, the first of these is internal prophetic dreams.

This kind of prophetic dream relates to your spiritual life. This is the type of dream that confirms where you are right now and gives you direction for the future.

The second is when you will receive a prophetic dream that relates to the Church Universal or to a specific ministry.

As you step out more in ministry, you will also receive dreams that will assist in helping others. Now, it can be a bit tricky sometimes to determine which dream fits into which group!

You do not want to interpret a dream for your church that is clearly for your personal ministry.

On the other hand, you do not want to interpret a dream meant for your church and apply it to a brother or sister. So how can you tell which dream is for whom?

Well, this chapter will help sort some of that out. Make a note of the checklists that I provide for you, under each group and apply them to your prophetic dreams. By now you have a good understanding of the Word and I will leave you to figure out the symbols.

For now, let us move on to taking the revelations the Lord is giving to you through dreams and using them in their correct context!

Now, keep in mind that we are speaking of prophetic dreams specifically here. So in each of these dreams, you are watching the dream from without! You are not the star of the show, but instead, a spectator in these dreams.

1. Personal Prophetic Dream

This dream is a representation of what is going on in your life right now and contains revelation regarding the future that God has for you.

As you go through the checklist below, you will notice how this group's main characteristic is that it consists of both character specific and universal symbols.

You will also note that you are actively involved in the dream. The part that makes it prophetic is that some of the symbols in this dream are universal. If it was a regular internal dream, you would not have any universal symbols in it.

Checklist

1. The dream is short and to the point.
2. You are an active participant in the dream.
3. Your emotions are likely to be active in the dream.
4. Some of the symbols are character specific.

5. Some of the symbols in the dream are universal.
6. You might hear words of prophecy. A phrase may be spoken in the dream.

Can you tick off every single one of these points? Then this dream relates to you specifically. Determine what is going on in your life right now. Let me remind you of the following questions, to determine the main point of the message the Lord is trying to get across to you right now.

- Is there something that you were praying for before you went to bed?
- Has the Lord been speaking to you about something specific in your journals lately?
- What were you reading or watching before you went to bed?

2. Prophetic Dream for the Church

It is important to know that the Lord will give you this kind of dream for a number of reasons. I consider Moses who was quite happy to spend the rest of his days on the backside of the desert. God had other plans though and when God's people began to pray, Moses had an encounter!

One of the most influential factors for you having a prophetic dream for the Church or a specific ministry is this – God's people have been praying! As you already know, a revelation should always be applied!

In Moses' case, his experience was a call to take action. In some cases, the Lord might just be calling you to intercession. Your dream might contain a warning that He wants you to share with a specific ministry.

The second most common reason for having such a dream, is that you have been seeking the Lord in this direction. Have you been praying for the Church lately? Has a specific ministry been on your heart during prayer? The Lord will give you revelation according to what you have been seeking Him for.

This dream is very common to those that have an evangelistic ministry. An evangelist could easily have a dream like this, which would speak specifically of a nation or a group of people.

Now, before you run off and decide that your dream is for the Church or a specific ministry, see if it lines up with the points listed below.

CHECKLIST

1. The dream is short and to the point.
2. You see it as if watching a movie.
3. You are not present or active in the dream at all.
4. There are *no* character specific symbols.
5. *All* of the symbols in the dream are universal.
6. You might hear words of prophecy. A phrase may be spoken in the dream.

A dream like this will be very clear and the symbols will be clear. A good example of this is the book of Revelation. Do you notice how John's visions for each church are so specific and confirmed by Scripture?

John is not in the visions, but he stands from without, looking at the things that are taking place. This is the same for a clear prophetic dream. You will dream of symbols that are very specific to the ministry that you receive the revelation for.

3. Prophetic Dream for Others

> *Daniel 2*
> *6 However, if you tell the dream and its interpretation, you shall receive from me gifts, rewards, and great honor. Therefore tell me the dream and its interpretation.*
>
> *Daniel 2*
> *19 Then the secret was revealed to Daniel in a night vision. So Daniel blessed the God of heaven.*

If ever I have seen abuse in the realm of dream interpretation it has to lie under this heading! I put it last, because you should try to determine the other two groups first.

It is vital that you try to interpret your dream internally first. If you have been praying for someone though, it is common for the Lord to give you a dream on their behalf.

Now, the characters will still be symbolic in such a dream, only the interpretation will not be for you, but for someone specific. I have had many dreams like this on behalf of my spiritual children and disciples.

There have been times when I have gone to bed with someone heavily on my heart. I might be praying, "Lord what is going on? What does this person need? What is going on in their lives?"

I did not "get" at first that the dreams that followed this prayer were for that person! I always tried to interpret them internally and could not figure out what was going on. I think that the hardest part is the presence of so many character specific symbols!

What Sets This Group Apart

There is one tiny point that I overlooked though. Even though many of the symbols were character specific, I was not active in the dream! I was always on the outside looking in.

This is such an important part to remember in your dreams. When you are not the star of your dream, it is prophetic! In other words, that dream is not for you, but for someone else!

When all of the symbols are universal, then that dream is for a ministry or the Church.

> **KEY PRINCIPLE**
>
> However, when the symbols are character specific to both you and someone you are praying for, then the interpretation is for them!

I think the most outstanding characteristic of this group is that you are on the outside watching, and that the symbols are character specific to both you and the person.

So if you have been praying for a friend and the Lord gives you a dream for them, firstly, you will be standing on the outside and watching events unfold. Secondly, the symbols in the dream will mean the same thing to both of you.

Knowing this really helps. If you feel that a dream might be for someone you know, then share it with them and ask what they feel the symbols in the dream might mean. If you share the same impression, then you can feel confident to also share your interpretation.

Let's see if I can help you out with the checklist.

CHECKLIST

1. The dream is short and to the point.

2. You see it as if watching a movie (You stand on the outside watching).
3. You might even be watching yourself perform specific acts.
4. You are not affected emotionally by what you see (You feel detached from the events).
5. The environment or circumstance of your dream will represent the person the dream is about.
6. Most of the symbols in the dream are character specific.
7. You will have some universal symbols.
8. You might hear words of prophecy. A phrase may be spoken in the dream.

WHO THE DREAM IS FOR – LOOK FOR MARKERS

Now, how can you tell who the dream is about, when you have determined that it is clearly not for you? A good place to start would be to consider who you were thinking about before going to bed, or who you are currently praying for.

There will also be clear markers in the dream that will lean to someone quite specific.

Say for example you have been praying for your father, and asking the Lord to reach him. Then that night you dream you are in your father's house, watching events unfold. Because it is in your father's house, you recognize all the symbols. Symbols you would both relate to.

This dream would be for your father. Either the Lord is shedding light on his problem so that you can help out, or you are meant to pray the problem through.

How about if you have been praying for a specific pastor? You have been asking the Lord to anoint him. Then that night you dream that you are in the church building and as you watch on, oil begins to pour over the pastor's pulpit. The interpretation is so clear!

The Lord is confirming that he will indeed pour out a fresh anointing on that pastor's ministry!

DANIEL

Let's take a page out of Daniel's book here. We all know of the incident when the king had a dream, but would not tell the wise men what it was. So Daniel sought the Lord and it says in Chapter 2 and verse 16, that the Lord revealed the same dream to him in a night vision!

In other words, Daniel had the same dream. In this moment, the king and Daniel shared the same symbols.

NOT ALWAYS FOR SHARING

It is encouraging when you are praying for someone and the Lord gives you just the right words to pray. Sometimes this dream will give you insight as to what is going on in that person. Often the dream will be a call to intercession and prayer.

You need to seek the Lord for wisdom about sharing the dream with the person in question. Not every revelation we receive as prophets is meant to be shared. More often than not, they are meant to be prayed through and applied. Before sharing a dream with someone that you feel is specific to them, follow the other steps you have learned so far regarding the correct timing and sharing with tact.

I hope that each of these groups has given you a guideline for where to apply your dream interpretation. Whether the Lord speaks to you using visions or in a dream, the point is not the revelation itself. Rather the point is that God's message gets out.

An unapplied revelation is an empty one. A word must be "sent" before it can be "accomplished." So even in this, realize that the Lord has not spoken to you just so that you might know something no one else does. Rather He intends for you to apply your revelation.

THE ONE RULE

Applying it might involve simply praying it through. It might involve sharing your dream with someone or even decreeing it at church. When to apply your revelation has only one rule – when God says so!

As you become familiar with receiving revelation through dreams, realize that the Lord will not keep you there. As you mature as a prophet you will move on to other ways of hearing His voice. I know that you cannot imagine it right now, but there are even more exciting ways that God can speak to you.

Why not dig into the next chapter to see what I am talking about!

CHAPTER 08

FUNCTIONING IN VISIONS

Chapter 08 – Functioning in Visions

2 Corinthians 12
1 It is doubtless not profitable for me to boast. I will come to visions and revelations of the Lord.

In this passage, it is clear that Paul was used to receiving visions from the Lord, but this way of hearing from Him is not restricted to the apostle alone. In fact, every believer can hear the Lord through visions. As a prophet though, you will function in this more than most.

I thrive on visions! Whether I am sharing this with you, preaching from the pulpit, playing a song, singing in the spirit, walking down the road, or talking to the Lord - I am living in visions.

It lines up with what I said concerning the signs of the prophetic calling in the *Prophetic Essentials* book. As prophets, we love to think in pictures. It is what prophets do. We love to think allegorically.

What's a Vision?

So what's a vision? Let me make it plain. A vision is simply a picture in your mind. What I love about visions is that they give you the next step along the road. The Word says that He is a lamp to our feet and a light to our path. (Psalms 119:105)

Visions are like the lamp, just there by your foot. Visions do not give you the full picture all at once.

You will find that when the Lord gives you revelation, He gives it to you a piece at a time. He doesn't offload the whole thing on you all at once. It comes a piece at a time. You are going to experience that He will give you one little picture, and as you receive and share that piece, you will receive more.

I want you to start experiencing visions in your private prayer times. Experience visions in your times with the Lord whether you are reading, talking to the Lord or submitting the day to Him. I want you to be sensitive to the pictures that He puts into your mind.

Learn to develop visions in your prophetic walk. This is the language of heaven. This is the language of the Lord. He speaks in pictures. Learn to identify them in every aspect of your life.

HOW THE PROPHET FLOWS IN VISIONS

Remember how I shared how man is made of spirit, soul and body? Well, visions are the Lord using your sense of sight – sending you a picture from your spirit. That is why most visions you receive, will come from deep within.

We will move to discussing different vision types shortly, but as a prophet, you will receive most of your revelation from within your spirit. You will not often receive your revelation from without.

Think about that for a minute because this is essential to how you hear from God as a prophet (especially if you are used to flowing more as an evangelist.) This is one main hindrance to flowing in visions, for someone moving into the prophetic.

The evangelist will hear from God externally. The revelations will be clear, and the vision and His voice will almost be external and loud. This is not so for the prophet. The Lord will speak to you gently from deep within your spirit.

The pictures and words you receive will come with impulses and deep impressions. They will be gentle and will flow like rivers of living water. So if you were used to hearing the clear words of God from without and flowed more evangelistically, then get used to the change!

THE GENTLE BREEZE OF JESUS

The main reason for this is the emphasis on your relationship with Jesus. The Holy Spirit although indwelling, moves externally. That is why in a revival meeting you will literally see the Holy Spirit move from without.

This is not the primarily realm of the prophet.

KEY PRINCIPLE

> You will flow with a different kind of anointing. We like to call it "the gentle breeze of Jesus." It is a gentle flow that starts from deep within and flows outwards.

It is the kind of anointing that melts hard hearts, heals broken hearts and inspires hopeless hearts. This is the core of who you are as a prophet and how you hear God speaking to you, will be in accordance with this relationship.

Jesus does not shout. He woos and inspires. So do not worry if you do not receive external visions that stop you dead in your tracks. You are a prophet - Jesus will whisper His secrets to you from deep within, like a groom forming the words of a love song.

VISION TYPES

Mark 4
33 And with many such parables He spoke the word to them as they were able to hear it

When Jesus walked the earth, He spoke in parables and pictures to illustrate His point. And in all these years, He hasn't changed. He loves to give us pictures. Why? We remember pictures. Pictures stick with us.

It is hard to remember a prophetic word, but it is easy to remember an illustration.

And so the Lord will put pictures in your mind. He will use visions to speak to you, and this is something that you can develop more and more.

If I hear a prophet that cannot function in visions, although it is possible, it is really strange and I think that they are doing themselves a disservice by not hearing from God in this way.

Key Principle

> It is great to go on impressions and the audible voice, but without visions, it's like being a blind man.

It's like saying, "Oh well, I am satisfied just to hear and feel what is going on around me - but I don't need to see the color. I don't need to see the blueness of the sky, the color of the rainbow, or the beautiful rich red of the rose. It's good enough for me to just smell it and feel it. I don't need to see it."

Now, who is that foolish in the natural? What blind man is happy to stay blind? Well, it is the same for the prophetic. If you don't flow in visions, trust me, you are like a blind man.

Visions are like taking a snapshot with your camera - it tells a story. I could sit here and try to explain to you what a rose looks like, or I could take a picture and you could see the colors for yourself.

What is going to be more effective? Well, it's the same in the spirit. You can understand the Word and get impressions from your spirit, but when you see visions in your spirit, it puts it all into place for you.

So, visions are a very important way of being able to hear the voice of God. Do you flow in visions? If so, develop it!

If you are not there yet, then do not be discouraged, because it is quite likely that you are flowing in this way already without realizing it.

THE THREE VISION CATEGORIES

1ST CATEGORY: PROPHETIC VISIONS

> *John 7*
> *38 He who believes in Me, as the Scripture has said, out of his heart will flow rivers of living water.*

This is by far, the category that the Holy Spirit uses most to speak to His people. I used the passage above because hearing God in this way feels very much like it describes.

These visions flow out from deep within, like rivers of water. This is probably the most difficult concept to grasp for many people, even though it is the easiest to master.

In fact, the Lord Jesus is speaking to you all the time in impressions and visions – you might just not recognize it. This is a struggle I have seen with so many prophets, who have come to us for training.

Used to hearing from the Lord externally, they wait for their visions to be suspended in front of them. They wait to fall into a trance before saying, "I received a vision from God!" Sure, God does speak in this way also, but it is not the primary method He uses.

Unfortunately, many have gone about seeking these experiences and have certainly found them… but not all can be accredited to the Holy Spirit! Have you ever wondered why deception is running rampant amongst the prophetic ministry? It is because of the continuous "searching" that prophets are doing for the open vision.

Rest assured that God is speaking to you right now, in visions. It is the most articulate language of the spirit, with sight being our strongest sense.

He speaks to us today, like He did to Apostle Paul, when he saw a Macedonian inviting him to come and preach to them. (Acts 16:9)

The Macedonian was a symbol of the people that God was sending him to.

Now, I cover interpreting symbols to your visions in my Dreams and Visions book, so I am not going to labor the point here.

Rather, I want to draw your attention to the fact that you are hearing God right now. Do you know those "impressions" you have seen when you pray? Those are visions!

When you are expecting to go into a trance or for the Lord to "slam" you with an open vision, you miss an important fact. You miss that you could be having a conversation with the Lord every moment of your day.

These visions are simple pictures that come from your spirit, leaving an impression on your mind. You might be journaling or praying with someone and you will get an "impression" of a river that is blocked. That is a vision!

When you "get it" that you have been seeing visions all along, a whole new world will open up to you. Then you can focus on that and expect it.

KEY PRINCIPLE

> Prophetic visions are pictorial impressions that come to your mind from your spirit.

2ND CATEGORY: TRANCE VISIONS

> *Acts 11*
> *5 I was in the city of Joppa praying; and in a trance I saw a vision, an object descending like a great sheet, let down from heaven by four corners; and it came to me.*

Our second category of visions is the kind that Peter had while waiting for lunch to be ready. This is a vision where your senses are suspended. You suddenly smell, feel or see things in the spirit that you are not feeling in the natural.

Your eyes are closed and it feels as if you are somewhere else. John G. Lake certainly operated in this very strongly, which is no surprise because he was an evangelist. He would pray for someone from a long distance, and see them being healed in the spirit, even though he was not there.

The scripture above is one of the very few instances where this type of vision is mentioned in the New Testament, which makes one think. When you consider the message of this vision, I understand why the Lord gave Peter a trance instead of just a simple prophetic vision.

Consider that in this vision Peter struggled with the Lord. He really did not want to hear this message! He tried to denounce it, but it was so strong, that he had to sit up and pay attention.

Had the Lord tried to give Peter this message as a prophetic vision, I can guess that he would have brushed it aside as his "imagination" and not thought about it further. However, God really had a point to make here.

He had to work through Peter's prejudice and open his eyes to a secret about the New Testament Church. Never once did it occur to Peter that salvation was also for the Gentiles... not until his vision, that is!

So clearly, God needed to make a point. I would daresay that those who often function in this vision type are people who God is trying hard to get His message across to.

KEY PRINCIPLE

> In a trance vision, the Lord suspends your senses, because He needs you to put your own ideas aside and listen to Him.

This is what Zacharias found out when he decided to argue with the angel that told him that he would be the father of John the Baptist! The Lord made such a point - he struck him dumb!

So if you have flowed in this kind of vision, take note because the Lord had a strong message for you that you were meant to obey. If you do not flow in this way, then you can take a deep breath of relief. Perhaps you are ready to hear God and not "brush aside" His message, and so He does not need to suspend your senses.

3rd Category: Open Visions

> *Numbers 24*
> *4 The utterance of him who hears the words of God, who sees the vision of the Almighty, who falls down, with eyes wide open:*

You will notice that open visions are only mentioned very rarely and then only in the Old Testament. There are a number of reasons for this. The first is that the Holy Spirit was not indwelling in the Old Testament.

When God spoke to man, He had to do so externally. He appeared when He willed and only for short periods of time. In the New Testament, we can hear God any time we need to!

Just imagine, in the Old Testament they did not have the luxury of an internal "Urim and Thummim." They had to schlep all the way to the High Priest to hear from God.

The same with visions – they had to wait for the Lord to come upon them to hear from Him. Looking at the scripture I include above, I find the reference to the open vision, surrounding an interesting occurrence.

What makes it interesting is that Balaam was a false prophet!

BALAAM

In fact, he had opened his mouth, ready to curse Israel and at the moment he opened his mouth to speak, God stepped in and took over. Instead of speaking that curse, with eyes wide open, he found himself looking over the tents of Israel. A completely different picture was superimposed over it.

In other words, his eyes were open, but what he saw was not the reality, but a picture God wanted him to see.

KEY PRINCIPLE

> The open vision is where a picture is superimposed over your natural senses. Your eyes see what God wants them to see – such as in the case of Balaam.

The Lord literally took Balaam over to make sure that His perfect will was spoken forth, instead of the curse.

I think it stands to reason, that if God has to take you over and shout at you so loudly… that you really are not terribly open to hearing His voice, and that you have your own agenda.

I am not saying that God does not speak in this way today – He is God, He can do what He pleases! I am saying that in our New Testament era that He does not need to shout, as He did in the past.

He does not need to wait for the perfect moment before resting upon us and bending us to His will. As His children and as His bride, He speaks to us from within. He has filled us with rivers of living water and He will flow out when He needs to.

Now, it is quite possible that the Lord could use this kind of vision, in an environment where a strong word needs to be spoken. It could be that the person He is speaking to needs to "get it" right down to the letter.

However, this is not normally the realm of the prophet and if you can flow more in prophetic visions, you will find your ministry leaping to the next level.

If Trance and Open Visions Stopped

If you flowed in trance and open visions and then they stopped, then do not be concerned! The Lord is not suddenly ignoring you. In fact, I would daresay that you got the message and you are open to hearing Him without Him having to shout.

I wish that I could say the same about good old Balaam though. He was so stubborn God made his donkey prophesy!

WATCHING FOR DECEPTION

I will say here though, that I am cautious of trance and open visions because of the way they have been used wrongly in the Church. Many of these "experiences" are often not of the Lord. I ministered to a pastor once who was born in a country where voodoo was commonplace.

Having been dedicated to the enemy as a young child, he always had strange experiences growing up. He said that even before he got born-again, he could astral travel around the house, while lying in bed at night. Trying to be a pastor and leader now for the Lord, he still had these experiences and they did not feel right to him.

He asked plainly, "Is this of God or not?" Well, the oppression in the room spoke for itself! Also, the experiences did nothing to glorify God or produce any faith, hope or love.

We confirmed for him that this "manifestation of the spirit" was not one from the Holy Spirit, but something completely demonic.

He could then renounce that and hear God clearly for the first time. The reason why I am cautious, when it comes to trance and open visions is that it is in the nature of the enemy to impose.

You see the Lord taking over Balaam – someone intent on doing His people harm. He did the same thing to

King Saul, who was intent on hurting David. However, you do not see Him having such a strong hand with those He loved and protected.

Unless they were fighting against His message, (such as with Peter) He invited them to hear His voice. The nature of the Lord Jesus is tender and inviting. It does not push.

KEY PRINCIPLE

> Jesus is the Good Shepherd, who leads, inviting us to follow. It is the butcher that drives and pushes the sheep from behind.

I believe that is why we see a distinct difference between how God spoke to the Old Testament saints to how He speaks to us today.

The indwelling of the Holy Spirit has changed everything. Where before only the select few could hear Him, the Scripture now says that:

> *Acts 2*
> *17 And it shall come to pass in the last days, says God, that I will pour out of My Spirit on all flesh; your sons and your daughters shall prophesy, your young men shall see visions, your old men shall dream dreams:*

The Spirit of God is now poured out on us all! Every single one of us can hear from God!

So weigh your revelations carefully and vet them through your mentor or spiritual leader. Hopefully, this has given you a good picture of what visions are and how to flow in them.

They are a powerful way to hear the Lord's voice and once you master this, the other four ways of how to hear the Lord, will build upon that foundation.

CHAPTER 09

FUNCTIONING IN TONGUES

Chapter 09 – Functioning in Tongues

> *1 Corinthians 14*
> *18 I thank my God I speak with tongues more than you all.*

I have had many opportunities in my life to learn different languages. In the country that I grew up in, there were eleven official languages. So depending on where you lived in the country, you would learn that region's tribal language.

Unfortunately, we moved around a lot, so I never really got to learn any of these languages properly. Every six months we went from one place to the other. I would just start learning a bit of one language and then we would move, and I would have to start all over again.

As a result, I must admit, I was left with some pretty bad impressions on how to learn a language. It seemed really hard for me, because I could never get the hang of it.

When I got a bit older and went into ministry, the Lord moved us to the opposite end of the world and I had to learn all over again. Now I was in a Spanish-speaking world and I had to learn some Spanish… at least enough to say, "Where is the bathroom?"

So I was faced with having to learn new languages again. Once I got over all my bad past experiences and fears, it actually became a lot of fun.

For most of us, learning a new language takes quite a bit of work. What is exciting though is when you finally get it right.

I experienced this for the first time in Europe when I could finally speak a bit of German. I went to Germany where I had my first full conversation with a local that I met there.

Okay sure, I was asking him about the chicken and how much it cost… but the point was, I could ask it in his native tongue! Even better – he actually understood me! It was so exciting. It lit such a fire in me, because I realized that I could communicate to a whole new world of people.

Suddenly languages became a very exciting thing.

THE LANGUAGE OF THE SPIRIT

Now when it comes to the world of the spirit, there is also a language that we have to learn and it is called speaking in tongues. What is exciting about speaking in tongues, is that you don't have to go through all that tough learning. You don't have to buy a library of books and audio-visuals.

Just like I had to learn to speak German to be able to communicate with a German speaking person - it is the same with the spirit. If you are going to understand the realm of the spirit and the messages of the spirit, you need to speak the language. That language is the gift of tongues.

This is a very special gift because it is not just about speaking the right things. Rather, it has the power to tap into your spirit and to do things in your spiritual life that you probably haven't even begun to understand.

I think that for people like me, who grew up in a charismatic, Pentecostal environment, speaking in tongues was the first thing you did. You got saved and then you spoke in tongues. It was just the way I grew up.

Unfortunately though, it becomes so commonplace that you lose the power that it has to transform your life.

Key Principle

> As a Christian, speaking in tongues is powerful. As a prophet it is invaluable.

You cannot walk your prophetic call out without speaking in tongues. It is one of the most important gifts that you need to possess. It is the starting point of all the other gifts of the Spirit.

Now, I am not going to get into a doctrinal controversy here and say that you are not saved if you cannot speak in tongues. I don't think that we need to take it and make a god out of it, separately from the Lord Jesus.

Simply put - without it you have a serious lack in your spiritual life.

It would be like going to war, lacking the power of the atom bomb and using a little peashooter against the enemy instead.

Speaking in tongues gives you the power that you need, to tap into the realm of the spirit. Not only that, but it also gives you the power to release what you have received from the Lord in the spirit.

PURPOSE OF SPEAKING IN TONGUES

As you start speaking in tongues, you get rid of all the junk and you start to fertilize your spirit. Once you have fed your spirit, you will have enough anointing to pour out to everyone else around you.

You really need to take that time. It is like a chef that spends all his time cooking and preparing food. There comes a time when he has to sit down and eat.

KEY PRINCIPLE

> There has to come a time in your spiritual walk when you stop and feed your spirit, so that you can feed others.

As a prophet, this applies to you even more so, because you should be walking in the realm of the spirit all of the time. People are looking to you for revelation and direction from the Lord. This means that you should always be in a place of pouring out.

The problem is, if you don't take the time to charge up, you will become spiritually weary and your "revelations" will start coming from your mind.

You will no longer feel the anointing - and this is the biggest problem of all. You will start to lack the anointing in your ministry. It is because you haven't taken the time to strengthen your spirit.

I hope I am challenging you to look back at the fundamentals. We get so caught up in ministering and doing the work, that we forget to stop and charge up again.

So with that being said, what really is the purpose of speaking in tongues?

1. Builds Your Spirit Up

Firstly, speaking in tongues builds up your spirit.

I had a couple of bodybuilders in my family on my mother's side. In fact, my grandfather was a keen weight training fanatic, right into his older years.

When we went on vacation together, instead of sleeping in like the rest of us, he was usually up at six or seven in the morning, at the gym, pumping weights.

I thought to myself, "That's the craziest thing. You are supposed to be taking a break. You are supposed to be chilling out." And there he was... at the gym.

But you know, that's why he looked the way he did. He was always building up his muscles. If ever he had to stop and not do it anymore, he would lose the power and strength in those muscles.

TAP INTO YOUR INNER BODYBUILDER!

Well, it is the same in the spirit. What you need to ask yourself is, "Is there a spiritual body builder inside of me or a weedy little nerd?"

Well, that depends on how much you have been building your spirit up. Don't think that because a year ago you were this big muscular, tough guy in the spirit that you are there today.

Unless you maintain it on a regular basis, you are going to lose that edge. Keeping your spirit fit is the same as in the natural - you have to keep going to the gym and put the effort in. When you put the effort in, you reap the fruits of it.

Do you want a nice, strong muscular spirit? Then you need to continue speaking in tongues and make it part of your daily life. Then you can be a big spiritual bodybuilder that is strong and muscular and ready to take on anything that comes your way.

2. Cleanses Your Spirit

One of the most exciting things about tongues and its most practical uses, is that it cleans out your spirit fast!

This is a powerful principle that is easily forgotten. You get so busy striving and trying to please the Lord that you get distracted. You forget that there is a very simple way to get back into His presence and to bring your spirit in line.

Key Principle

> You can get spiritually fit again, by just taking time to speak in tongues.

Have you been distracted? Perhaps you have had a tough week and all hell has broken loose against you. Speaking in tongues gives you the life you need.

Perhaps you are frustrated and you are battling to hear the voice of the Lord. You think to yourself, "Was that the Lord or was it my imagination?"

Speaking in tongues brings your spirit to life. It separates the dross from the gold. It comes with a dividing line. It separates the spirit from the flesh, like oil and water.

Sometimes things can look a little bit mixed up and you don't know what's the flesh and what's the spirit, because it is all so confused. Speaking in tongues brings that clear division.

Speaking in tongues is like drilling through rock to sink a pipe into an underground stream, for the purpose of setting up a windmill. Once the windmill is all set up, all you need is for the wind to blow and the living water springs up from the ground.

Getting to that point though takes a bit of effort. The best way to make sure you have God's fresh water on tap is to speak in tongues for periods of time.

SETTING UP YOUR WINDMILL

Now, perhaps your pipe has gotten a little bit clogged along the line. It has gotten a bit jammed up with stress, the fight that you had with your spouse, the struggles you are having at work and the conflicts you are having at church. Through it all, you get plugged up and contaminated.

At first you don't realize it, but slowly you notice that you have lost "the edge" when you minister. Don't think that your spirit is always free, because you are in ministry all the time.

Sometimes you can get so hung up on doing the work of the ministry and on pouring out that you can get clogged up and dull in your spirit, because you have forgotten to tap into the life source.

If you have been running around, ministering to others and pouring out of the portion that you have, after a while, the chances are, you are going to start feeling a little bit dry.

You will start pouring out from your intellect. You will begin to rely on what you know in your head. You will stop giving people the life of the spirit that is inside of you and swap it out for a bunch of rotten manna.

Speaking in tongues changes all of that. It allows you, firstly to get your mind out of the way. When you put in the effort, you are not sitting, concentrating on cares and problems, and coming up with logical solutions. Secondly it starts to tap into the stream of life inside of you.

This is what Jesus meant when He said:

> *John 7*
> *38 He who believes in Me, as the Scripture has said, out of his heart will flow rivers of living water.*

USES FOR SPEAKING IN TONGUES

One of the best ways to use speaking in tongues, is for the purpose of spiritual warfare. There are times when you come to minister to people and you don't have the answers.

1. SPIRITUAL WARFARE

You don't have the right words and you come into confrontation with demonic forces or with problems.

There is nothing sharper and more powerful than using tongues when you take authority over the enemy.

Tongues is a powerful tool, not only to build up your spirit, but to stand against the enemy as well. Remember, speaking in tongues is a spiritual language. Like I mentioned at the beginning, it is the language of the spirit. Trust me - the devil understands it very well.

Sometimes, especially when you are personally under attack, you don't have the strength to say. "Devil, go away, in Jesus' name…" You get tongue-tied and you get frustrated.

That's exactly what tongues is for. Get your mind out of the way and just speak as God would speak to him. There is a power in that, and you will feel the tongues coming out of your spirit as you take authority over the enemy.

Now, you might not know what you said to him, but you know it was good, because you felt an atom bomb go off in the spirit. The Lord has a way of saying things that you don't know how to say.

2. Issuing Decrees

Also, use tongues to speak forth decrees, because the angels know what you are saying. There are times, actually very often in intercession, when you will have a desire to speak an utterance. You will feel the authority and the gift of faith rising up inside of you and in that moment you should speak out the decree.

In moments like these, you may not know exactly what you said, but you knew that there was power there. Well, you just released something in the spirit. You gave the angels license in the earth, to do what God wanted them to do.

You don't always have to do everything yourself. You don't have to rely on your own understanding all the time. That is why God has given us tongues, so we don't have to rely on our limited knowledge and ability.

3. Releasing Angels

It is also used to release angels in the spirit. David got this concept when he wrote,

> *Psalms 103*
> *20 Bless the Lord, you His angels, who excel in strength, who do His word, heeding the voice of His word.*

Angels are used of the Lord to do His bidding. So it stands to reason, that the only time, angels are going to do anything on your behalf, is when they hear God's word come forth from your lips!

They understand your tongues and when you are speaking words out of your spirit, directed by the Holy Spirit, you can be sure that action will follow.

Trust me, they understand what you are saying. When you speak in faith, whether you speak in your native tongue, a language you just learned, or you are speaking in tongues - they understand. They understand the force of faith that comes with it.

So imagine a group of angels just hanging out in the Throne Room of God. The worship angels are singing and the warrior angels are gathered around the coffee machine (It's heaven, of course it must have coffee right?!)

The next thing you know, a voice echoes through the air and the angels pick up their swords and say, "Did you guys hear that? I heard the Father utter a command! We better get moving to obey!"

Well that tongue-in-cheek picture there, is what happens when you speak the words of God! Angels do not move until they hear the Father. When you pray in the spirit and the Holy Spirit directs you, you can be sure that angels and demons alike hear your words.

In fact, I enjoy speaking in tongues more than in English in spiritual warfare, because I do not need to try and wax eloquent. I can simply let God speak in my stead!

THE ANOINTING IS VITAL

Now, before you think that just any of your tongues hold that kind of power – think again. Without the anointing, your words mean nothing. You can know all the principles and you can know the Word from cover to cover, but without the anointing, you are not making a difference in people's lives. You are not making a difference in the realm of the spirit.

Speaking in tongues is one of the best and most effective ways to tap into that anointing. It is the perfect way to make sure, whether you speak English or tongues that it comes gushing out with fresh water.

CHAPTER 10

FUNCTIONING IN UTTERANCE AND INTERPRETATION

Chapter 10 – Functioning in Utterance and Interpretation

> *1 Corinthians 14*
> *5 I wish you all spoke with tongues, but even more that you prophesied; for he who prophesies is greater than he who speaks with tongues, unless indeed he interprets, that the church may receive edification.*

Now, there comes a time though when you can't always speak in tongues. There comes a time when you have to speak English.

It is great when a bunch of prophets get together and you can carry on in tongues for hours. In fact, you can all have a wonderful time and share in the presence of the Lord.

Apostle Paul said though, in the passage above, "Guys, if you are in a public meeting and you speak in tongues, you have to speak out the utterance. You have to speak it in the native tongue, so that everybody there can be edified and the Lord can reveal what is in their hearts."

If you have the opportunity in a local church, it is a great place for you to apply this principle. If you are new to utterance and interpretation though, then the best way for you to "get into the flow", is to do so in your prayer closet.

In fact, this is the way I learned to interpret my own tongues. I did so in the privacy of my prayer closet, where the only ones to bear the brunt of my fumbling and mistakes was the pile of laundry I had yet to pack away.

The Difference Between Utterance and Interpretation

Now, before I speak more on how to flow in utterance, let me interrupt myself here quickly and clarify the difference between utterance and interpretation. The secret lies in the following passage:

> *1 Corinthians 14*
> *27 If anyone speaks in a tongue, let there be two or at the most three, each in turn, and let one interpret.*

Key Principle

> To put it plainly – an utterance is a flow of inspired tongues that comes from your spirit. Interpretation is the interpretation of those tongues in your native language.

Perhaps you have seen this in effect at a meeting. I sure grew up with it all my life. Someone would stand up during worship and belt out a confident string of inspired tongues. Followed by that was a strong silence as everyone wondered, "Who will bring the interpretation?"

Then followed, the sigh of relief as the "usual guy" stood up and interpreted. The sigh of relief stemming from - "Whew! I am glad the guy giving that utterance did not miss it." Mixed with, "Whew I am glad that God did not call on me to bring the interpretation!"

My First Interpretation

Of course, back then I was just the pastor's kid and was allowed to hide in the background a bit. Things changed though when I started becoming involved in the ministry.

I remember one of the first times that God tapped me on the shoulder to bring the interpretation. It happened in a public meeting, back in the early days when I was still learning to prophesy. I was still getting the hang of what utterance and all this stuff was.

The leader (my Dad) gave the utterance in bold confidence. Then… silence. I looked around thinking, "I wonder who has the interpretation."

He was waiting for the interpretation and thinking, "Okay guys, any minute now somebody is going to give it."

It was then that I felt that all too familiar "butterflies in my stomach" feeling, indicating that the Lord was giving me something. I was so nervous and I sat and waited… and waited.

After agonizing, for what felt like forever, I finally stepped out and gave the interpretation.

After the meeting, my dad said, "Here is a new rule: If I give the utterance, have your mouth open and ready to interpret by the time I am done." That seemed to be a lot of pressure, but actually it was a really good point. One I kept for my team's training. Obviously, if God is giving a message in tongues, He expects it to be interpreted!

How to Interpret Effectively

So from that time on, every time somebody in the meeting started with the utterance, I did not wait until they finished. I said, "Okay Lord, have you given me the interpretation?" Sometimes it was a "yes" and sometimes it was a "no." However, the point is, I didn't sit and wait and then say somewhere along the line, "Oops, they are finished, do you want me to bring the interpretation Lord?"

(In the meantime 15 minutes have passed and everybody is still waiting…)

I know that this is a common mistake, so this is a practical tip if you are working with a team, or are in a local church with more than one prophet.

Jump In!

If, somebody starts bringing the utterance in tongues, don't wait for them to finish, before asking the Lord if He has given you the interpretation.

Obviously there is an interpretation - otherwise there wouldn't have been an utterance in the first place. So when they start speaking in tongues - that's the moment to ask the Lord, "Do I have the interpretation?"

Usually, if I step into that place and make myself available, I almost immediately get a vision, or the first few words of the interpretation, so that the moment they finish, I can step in.

There are times though when I don't have it. In which case I can sit back, chill out and relax and let somebody else bring the word.

Learning to Flow in Utterance and Interpretation

The key though with all of this, again and again, is to do it in your private, prayer closet first. Don't feel pressured into thinking that you have to be a big hotshot out there.

You know, you can practice this in your quiet time with the Lord and learn to develop this ability. Prophesy over yourself. Prophesy over your children. Speak in tongues and pray for people you know well. Develop it.

Take your time. Learn to become familiar with this language of the spirit.

When I first started learning how to speak a different language in the natural, I wasn't so arrogant that I went out immediately to find a German speaking person, and try to hold a conversation - with the whole two German words I knew.

Some people are that arrogant and they are annoying. I didn't want to be annoying. I wanted to make sure I could at least speak a sentence, that they could understand.

Do the same with the spirit. Learn a bit. Take the time to get to know the realm of the spirit. Take your time to get to know the voice of the Lord.

Then when you step out, you are going to do it with confidence. You are going to have good experiences, not bad experiences that are going to leave you feeling discouraged.

SING IN TONGUES

A fantastic way to learn to interpret your tongues, is to praise and worship in tongues during your private times with God. As prophets, we have the ability to release the anointing through music. If you want to take your spiritual life to a new level, try interpreting your tongues by singing with your guitar, play on your piano or sing while you are driving your kids to school (if they can bear it).

Take the time to interpret your tongues while you are singing. Sing it out. It is a fantastic first step to learn how to prophesy in song, and it is something that I learned to do a very long time ago.

I can't actually remember when it was, because it became such a part of my life and ministry.

Every time you worship, you can guarantee that there is going to be something new waiting for you in the spirit. So give that a try and you will be amazed at the sudden increase of anointing.

There is something about music (We will look at prophetic music in the next book in the series). When you combine tongues, music, and interpretation, there is such power there. So give this a try in your next prayer time and see what happens. Soon you will be raving about it just as much as I am.

Tongues, utterance, and interpretation are a powerful way to hear God's voice. In fact, the more time you spend in the Word and in the Spirit, the more you can expect to hear God in this way.

Keep in mind that each of these ways of hearing God is geared towards the prophetic ministry. There are certainly other ways to hear from God as well, but as a prophet, the chapters in this book are your "red phone line" to the King of Kings!

CHAPTER 11

FUNCTIONING IN PROPHECY

Chapter 11 – Functioning in Prophecy

> *1 Thessalonians 5*
> *20 Do not despise prophecies.*

I had the wonderful opportunity once to go on a hot air balloon. I had a friend whose parents had a sideline business. Over weekends, they would take people up in a balloon for a champagne breakfast. It was very popular with honeymooners.

After tagging along over weekends for some time, we were allowed to go for a ride of our own.

I wasn't sure what I was quite expecting - perhaps a big rush - but it was really different to what I thought it would be.

One of the first things I realized, when we went up, was that I felt as if I was standing on air. It was the most amazing thing. Even though I had the basket around me, I didn't feel afraid or insecure. I felt safe.

The other thing that I didn't realize, (even though it is quite logical when you think about it) is that when you are in a hot air balloon, you can't dictate which direction you go in. You are at the mercy of the wind.

You only hold the power to get in the basket and turn on the burners. Once you are in the air though, that's it. You are at the mercy of the wind.

The way this couple did it, is that one person would be in charge of the balloon, and the other would follow it on the road in a truck. This way, wherever they landed, they could meet up.

When it comes to speaking out a prophetic word, it is a lot like taking a hot air balloon ride.

All you can do is get in the basket, fire up the burners, get into the air, and wait for the wind to blow. Then enjoy the ride, because the rest is up to the Holy Spirit.

The Truth About Prophecy

This is a lovely illustration of a prophetic word because it is a perfect picture of you and the Lord working together. You have your part and then the Lord has His. Your part is very simple. You just need to come to a place of making yourself available.

Then it is up to Him to blow the wind. If He doesn't blow it, you are not going anywhere. If He does blow it, you move in His direction.

You are out of control and that is a scary place to be for some people, but it is the best place to be for a prophet. There is nothing better than having the Lord in control.

You Are Not the Wind

There are times the wind just doesn't blow. You step up to the plate and make yourself available, but nothing happens. God decides to go on vacation and leave you holding the baby.

So there you stand, in the middle of the field, nicely suspended in the air, all ready to go… but going nowhere fast. What do you do?

It is such a common trend amongst some ministries to just step out, open your mouth and prophesy whatever comes out. To just prophesy and prophesy until something comes.

That would be like me standing under the hot air balloon, taking a deep breath and trying to use my own strength to create the wind, waiting for something to happen.

Listen… you are not the source of the wind. You are just the vessel.

KEY PRINCIPLE

> The wind comes from the Holy Spirit. It is for Him to blow and for you to make yourself available.

You got it a bit mixed up here. You cannot say, "Let's jump in there and give the prophetic word and hope that somewhere along the line, the anointing suddenly kicks in."

By God's grace, sometimes it does and you breathe a sigh of relief. If you keep pushing on that way though, you are just pushing on with your mind and what comes out is going to be a load of garbage, logic and human understanding.

A Prophet Does not Just Prophesy

I have seen so much damage done in the body of Christ when it comes to prophecy. So much to the point, I didn't want to write this chapter. Unfortunately, in many places prophecy has become the mark of the prophet.

That teaching says, "The prophet just prophesies."

The prophet doesn't just prophesy! When I read both the Old and the New Testament, the prophet did a lot more than that. When Nathan the prophet came to David concerning his affair with Bathsheba, he didn't just give David a prophetic word, He gave direction.

He shared a parable. He told David what the Lord had revealed to him. He didn't just prophesy all the time. They spoke like real people.

Even when Samuel spoke to Saul, he told him plainly what had happened to his donkeys, and what would happen to him on the way home (1 Samuel 10). He spoke with the Spirit. He didn't prophesy everything that He spoke.

Prophecy does hold a very powerful and vital part in the life of a prophet, so I don't want to swing you too much to the other extreme either.

KEY PRINCIPLE

> Do more than prophesy – speak with the Spirit!

I hope to bring you to a bit of balance. Prophecy is simply one tool in your tool belt.

USING PROPHECY CORRECTLY

By the end of this chapter, you will have the wisdom you need to flow in prophecy correctly. You will learn that being effective does not mean standing up and prophesying the first thing that comes to your head!

I have seen the most ridiculous things in prophetic ministry. I have heard some prophets say to someone needing ministry, "What profession are you in?"

"I am a brick layer."

"Well, just as you are brick layer in the natural so the Lord is calling you to lay bricks for the Church of God and …"

Are you serious? That is like standing under the balloon and huffing and puffing, trying to make the wind.

Here is a little tip... let God blow the wind. You climb into the basket and fire up the burners, then leave the rest up to Him.

You are already pumped up by speaking in tongues, you already have a face-to-face relationship with the Lord Jesus – now it is just a case of, "Lord here I am - I make myself available to you."

It won't take long and the Lord will blow the wind.

When it comes to speaking out a prophetic word, this is not the time for you to make things up. When you are journaling, you have the liberty to mess things up.

When you are busy practicing at home and you are feeling your way around, it is okay to make things up a bit to get yourself going.

If you mess it up while in your prayer closet, it is just you that has to suffer. When it comes to prophesying over other people, you don't have that luxury of making things up – because it is their lives on the balance now.

PROPHECY – STEP 1 AND 2

What happens if you make yourself available and nothing happens? That is why I want to give you some tips and hints here, of how to deal with it. I also want to help you to become confident in speaking out prophetic words. So let's get to it then!

Step 1. Make Yourself Available

Making yourself available is like getting into the basket. It means putting yourself in a place to be used by the Lord. Remember what I shared in the previous chapter about asking the Lord, "Do I have the interpretation Lord?"

Well, this is the same thing. It means deliberately putting yourself in a place to be used by Him. If there is a need, you are the first to ask the Lord, "Want me to say something Lord?"

So many believers think that God will throw them over His shoulder, and dump them into the basket, forcing them to participate. Remember, the Lord Jesus is a gentleman - He is not going to drag you through the streets by your hair like a caveman!

> ### *Key Principle*
> When God wants you to prophesy, He will wait for you to put yourself in place. Make yourself available. Ask Him to use you and once you do that the revelation will flow.

You will see a vision, receive the first words to a prophecy or hear something in the spirit.

STEP 2. OPEN YOUR MOUTH

It is only when you open your mouth though that you fire up the gas, light it and slowly ascend into the air.

Until you open your mouth and speak out what God gives you, you will not get any further direction. Opening your mouth is like turning on the burner.

And there, as you start to ascend, the wind is going to blow and your prophetic word will change direction.

Perhaps you are in a public meeting or in personal ministry and somebody needs direction from the Lord. You make yourself available by saying, "Lord, here I am. I am available."

At that moment, you might get a vision. Perhaps you will just get a few words, "I am with you…" That's all you get.

It's seldom that the Lord will give you a full sentence when it comes to prophecy. He gives you the first few words or perhaps just an impression in your spirit.

Perhaps as you are praying for someone, you sense that the road that the person is walking, on leads in the wrong direction. The Lord will not clarify or show you anything else – just that one piece.

THIS IS WHERE FAITH COUNTS!

What are you supposed to do with that? Well, then open your mouth. Until you open your mouth, you are not going anywhere. If you are sitting and waiting for the full revelation and picture, then let me break the news to you… it is not coming!

You have to step out in faith and say, "Thus saith the Lord! The part of the road that you are going down right now is going to lead you to destruction, but I have something better for you…"

The direction will come, the revelation will come, the wind will begin to blow, and you will start feeling a flow. Then it is up to the wind. In the next chapter I am going to give you things to remember, or avoid, when prophesying. For now though, you have just two things to do:

1. Make yourself available!
2. Open your mouth and speak.

The rest is up to the Holy Spirit.

CHAPTER 12

BREAKING PROPHECY DOWN

Chapter 12 – Breaking Prophecy Down

There are some simple guidelines to follow when prophesying. So in true form, I will break it down nicely for you, so that you are never left without the "know how" ever again!

Get Yourself in the Basket

So there you are in a ministry situation and you have made yourself available to the Lord.

You get an impression in your spirit. Perhaps you see a winding road in the spirit - a difficult road. When you see it, you know, "Ah, that's what the word is about." Or perhaps you hear the words, "The road has been difficult…"

That's all you get! Well, you are only going to fire up those burners when you open your mouth and you speak those first words. When you are new at it, you may fumble a bit, actually even when you are comfortable with it, you still fumble sometimes.

I think that the Lord allows us to mess up every so often, just to keep us humble!

That's when you fire up the burner, and then you will sense the flow of the spirit, and the words will come and come and then suddenly, they will stop.

Don't "Ride" the Anointing

That's the part where you shut up. I know, some prophets get so excited that God is using them, that when God stops blowing the wind, they carry on pushing with their own little bits that they always wanted to tell the pastor.

They cannot help but try to get in the juicy bits, that he was not willing to listen to before. They try to ride the anointing.

You try to ride the anointing to get in everything that has been on your mind for ages now.

> ### Key Principle
> No adding your own bits to prophecy! When the revelation stops - then you stop.

Get out of the basket. It is over. The ride is over! Finished!

When God Goes Quiet

There are times though when God grows quiet all of a sudden. Many prophets who come to us for training experience this.

They say to me, "I came, I made myself available, and there was no interpretation. I didn't get a prophetic word. I didn't get a revelation. Why didn't I get a revelation? Why didn't God move?"

The answer is simple. Why didn't you receive a revelation? Well, maybe there just wasn't one to get!

Maybe the person that you were ministering to didn't have faith. You are just a vessel. You are not the originator.

There is such a pressure on ministers at the moment, especially if somebody mentions the word "prophet."

"Obviously, if you are called a prophet then you always have a word to give."

ONLY SPEAK WHEN GOD SPEAKS

I read in 2 Kings 3 of the incident where three kings came together. The king of Israel, the king of Judah, and the king of Edom came together to fight and they said, "We need to hear from the Lord."

So they called good old Elisha out and they asked, "Should we go into the battle?" Elisha was not terribly impressed, it was clear that he did not think much of Jehoram.

He said, "If it weren't for the king of Judah, I wouldn't even have come to speak to you!"

He didn't just get up and give a prophetic word, but instead he said, "Bring me a psalmist. Bring me somebody to come play the harp."

He relaxed and as the music played, he got the prophetic word.

This was a mighty prophet. You would think that he would be in the spirit all the time and ready to belt out a prophetic word on demand, "Thus saith the Lord..."

However, even he could not speak unless God had spoken. Even such a mighty man of God had to wait and listen intently. As he waited on the Lord and made himself available, the Lord gave him the word and he spoke it. Sure enough, it came to pass just as he said it would.

KEY PRINCIPLE

> Don't ever feel under pressure to perform. You can only speak when God speaks.

It is tough sometimes though, especially when somebody has come to you with a need. It is a challenge when you are in a meeting and everybody is looking at you to "bring the word." On the inside, you are cringing and thinking, "I don't have a thing, guys."

In moments like these, there is a temptation to just make something up or to ride on the wave of somebody else's revelation. Don't ever feel insecure if God didn't speak to you – if the wind didn't blow.

The important thing, is that you got into the balloon. If the wind didn't blow, it is not your fault.

PROPHECY AND FAITH

Our walk is one of faith. It is one of God reaching down to man and not man reaching out to God. It is what makes our Christian walk, even as believers, different from every other religion out there.

Our religion is based on the fact, that while we were yet sinners He gave us His grace.

Your prophetic walk is based on the fact, that you are the most pathetic, useless, loser that God could find.

Your calling depends on His ability to speak to you and not on your ability to hear His voice.

KEY PRINCIPLE

> It is not your ability to hear God's voice that makes you a prophet. It is God's ability to speak to you and to raise you up with a prophetic anointing, that makes you a prophet.

Every believer should be able to hear God's voice because He is speaking to us all the time.

When it comes to ministry and to giving a prophetic word, it is for God to speak. That's why He is God. He is the originator. You are not the originator. Have you got my point yet?

GIVING GOD CONTROL OF PROPHECY

There are times when God will not speak. He is God… He is allowed to do that.

It is not for you to say, "God, I need a prophetic word, everybody is looking at me."

Who are you? You are just a clay pot. If the master doesn't want to pour wine in you and pour you out again, that is up to Him. It is for the Master to decide.

Sometimes we forget that. We get so full of the grace of the Lord and the fact that He will always just be there. We get so used to that fact that He will use these gifts, that we forget that He is a very sovereign and righteous God, who has a will of His own.

When He wills, He does what He wants and it is not for you to push the hand of God, and force Him to speak when He does not wish to speak.

He is a very holy God. He is a God that should be held in fear and respect, just as He is regarded with love and adoration. Until you have fear and respect for our

Heavenly Father you are going to give the wrong impression to the body of Christ.

When you have that godly fear and respect for the Lord, and you do speak a prophetic word, you are going to speak it on His behalf. You will know that the word is coming from the Throne Room - it is not coming from your mind. You are not just another "prophet" spouting the first thing that comes to your head.

HAVE THE COURAGE TO BE DIFFERENT

Be different! Stop comparing yourself with everyone else that is prophesying.

It reminds me of Elisha in 2 Kings 3 again when all the other prophets were prophesying, "Go forth, you will be victorious…"

They were giving their big, fanciful prophetic words and Elisha was the only one who had the courage to say, "Actually, the Lord says that you will not win this battle, you will be slain. You will not survive this day."

Guess whose word came to pass? The prophets who spoke the first thing that came to their heads - or the one that spoke from the Throne Room of God?

> **KEY PRINCIPLE**
> A true prophet speaks from the Throne Room of God – not from their own ideas.

Which one are you going to be? What is more important to you; to speak the truth or to have everybody say, "Well, he is such a mighty prophet, he can just prophesy anytime he wants"?

No, you can't prophesy any time you want. You prophesy when God speaks. If God doesn't speak, it might feel uncomfortable, but it is what will separate you from a prophetic "wannabe" and being a true prophet of God.

WHAT TO DO IF GOD DOES NOT SPEAK

Now that I have drilled the point home, I promise not to leave you hanging! I know how uncomfortable it is to stand in a meeting, or be faced with someone with an urgent need, only for God to grow ominously silent!

So let me give you a few lessons I learned for myself in this process. Hopefully, as you apply these points, you will feel more confident and also have the courage to only speak when you get a revelation.

All is not lost though if God grows quiet. There is a way to save face and still look like you know what you are doing! The prophet faces enough humiliation in his lifetime, without having to look like he has "lost it" in the middle of a meeting.

So gather around and take some notes, because you never have to feel lost ever again!

1. Speak in Tongues

The first thing, you can do, is speak in tongues - especially when you are in personal ministry.

If you bring the situation to the Lord and He does not answer, simply speak in tongues and let your spirit pray to God until you feel a release.

This is a wonderful way to say, "Okay Lord, it is in your hands. Your will be done."

Maybe the person you are ministering to is not ready for the revelation yet. Maybe it is not time. Let God be in control of the direction that the balloon goes in.

2. Release Blessing

The next thing you can do is to speak blessing. As a believer, you have the authority to speak blessing in the name of Jesus.

The Lord has given us the authority on this earth, just as He gave it to Adam, to speak things into existence, to speak blessing, and to speak His will according to the Word.

Say, for example, that you have somebody who has come to you with a marital problem. It could be a wife who feels that her husband is having an affair. Perhaps it is a husband struggling with something his wife is doing.

You bring the situation to prayer and… you get nothing.

You are thinking, "Lord, what do I do here?" As a prophet and as a believer you can speak blessing.

You can say, "Lord, you know the care that my brother or sister is facing right now, and I just speak your blessing on this situation.

I know that according to your Word, marriage is of you, so I stand against the enemy on behalf of my brother and I pray that you will bring your hand now, to bring reconciliation."

You might not have received a "Thus saith the Lord", but you can certainly pray according to the word He has already given us in the Scriptures!

3. STAND ON THE WORD

Say for example, that somebody comes to you with a physical or spiritual need. The Lord does not show you a thing! No vision, no prophetic word… never mind any wind, you do not even get a gentle breeze!

What now? The Word is clear and it stands true. You can speak peace into their situation. You can do as

Jesus did and speak to the winds and the waves, "Peace be still!"

Somebody comes to you with a financial problem. They keep having problem after problem and they don't know what is going on. They need revelation and you get no revelation. This does not mean that you cannot minister to them in love.

You can say, "Lord, I know it is not your will for your children to suffer. The Word says Lord that you will meet our needs according to your riches in glory. You are a giver of good gifts.

I speak blessing on these finances. I speak prosperity, so that everything their hand touches will prosper, just as you say in the Word."

Do you see the importance of all the bulldozing that I taught you about in the *Prophetic Essentials* book? So even if you don't get the revelation, it doesn't mean you can't pray. You can pray the prayer of faith just like it instructs us to do in:

> *James 5*
> *15 And the prayer of faith will save the sick, and the Lord will raise him up. And if he has committed sins, he will be forgiven.*

FIND A BALANCE

You don't always have to sit and wait for the revelation to come before you pray. You need to find a balance.

You have those that are always just prophesying a bunch of fluff every five minutes. Their words are like cotton candy that melts in your mouth – there is no lasting memory or effect.

And then you have others, that because they didn't get any revelation, step back and do not minister at all!

A crisis happens and you didn't get the revelation, so you just don't pray? Find a balance.

KEY PRINCIPLE

> If you don't get any revelation, pray according to the Word of God, because God gave enough revelation from Genesis to Revelation, for you to pray plenty.

When you stand on the Word in faith, the Scripture says,

> *Mark 11*
> *23 For assuredly, I say to you, whoever says to this mountain, 'Be removed and be cast into the sea,' and does not doubt in his heart, but believes that those things he says will be done, he will have whatever he says.*

It doesn't say, "And whoever gets a revelation can say to this mountain… "

It says, "Whoever says with faith to this mountain, be removed, it will be done."

It is very simple. God is the one who heals our disease. So, I didn't get a revelation, and I didn't feel any anointing. It doesn't mean that I can't stand on the Word of God and speak it.

Learn to make yourself available. Learn to get in that basket, and when you get the revelation and you get those words, speak them out. Fire up those burners and let the wind blow.

Let God be in control, and your prophetic words will go to a whole new level.

Chapter 13

General vs. Personal Prophecy

Chapter 13 – General vs. Personal Prophecy

There is a lot of confusion about the difference between personal and general prophecy. So once again, pick up your notebook and make some notes of these points.

I promise this will bring such a release in the way you minister as a prophet. Sometimes just knowing the "what, when and how" of these two prophecy types makes delivering them so much easier.

The General Prophecy

> *Acts 15*
> *32 Now Judas and Silas, themselves being prophets also, exhorted and strengthened the brethren with many words*

Hearing general prophecies are fun because they are given to a group. I say that they are fun, because they inspire everybody! The reality is that hardly anyone remembers them, but that is okay. The people leave the meeting feeling, "Yes, I heard from God".

Key Principle
> General prophecies are given to a group of believers.

They are the kind of words described in Acts 15:32.

They can have a few messages in them, but they relate to more than one person. If you are in a public meeting, this is the kind of prophetic word that you will receive.

GENERAL PROPHECIES ARE MOTIVATIONAL

Another characteristic of a general word is that it is usually motivational. The Lord will say to a group, "You are going in the right direction. I know that you are going through a tough time right now, but I am there for you and I am going to hold onto you. I am going to get you through it."

They are the kind of words that you need to hear straight from the Lord. Words like, "I am there for you. Hang in there."

Never stop giving these, because they uplift the body of Christ. They produce faith, hope and love.

General prophecies are there to help us go for a little while longer. Every now and again you need to hear the Lord say, "Hang in there. I am not going to let you go. I am there to help you through. Don't get discouraged."

That is not to say that a general prophecy cannot also issue a warning, or be directional. The Lord might also be saying to a group, "Don't allow the enemy to put bitterness in your heart. Let it go."

We all need that quick conviction every so often! We need it just like we need some tasty ice cream, every now and again on a hot summer's day, just to feel good.

We need that good stuff. It makes our life worth living. Sure, you cannot base your life on them, but it is these sweet moments that give you what you need to press on through.

PERSONAL PROPHECY

> *2 Samuel 12*
> *7 Then Nathan said to David, "You are the man! Thus says the Lord God of Israel: 'I anointed you king over Israel, and I delivered you from the hand of Saul,*

Now on the other side we have the personal prophecy. What makes this different, is that personal prophecy is a specific word given to an individual – just like we see here in 2 Samuel 12:7.

Very often it is quite personal which is why it is called "a personal prophecy!" It is personal to the person receiving it. It will touch on things that they might want to keep hidden, or on things that are hurtful.

Nathan did not walk through the streets of Israel and declare this word and what would happen – he had a private audience with David.

You don't stand up in the middle of a crowd and say, "Thus saith the Lord, your marriage is in trouble."

"You are living in sin."

"God is going to bring you to death."

"You have hurt from an abuse of the past, which God wants to heal."

There are just some things that do not need to be broadcast in front of the entire congregation!

Let's raise up prophets who have the wisdom to give the personal prophecy, to the person it is intended for.

CHANGE THE TREND!

Let's change the trends a little. There have been times when God has led me to single somebody out in a public meeting and say, "Rise up. Don't allow the enemy to steal God's blessing from you."

However, more often than not, I share a word like that in a private setting, after the meeting. If that is not possible, the Lord arranges circumstances where I can minister to them personally.

NO MORE "DRIVE BY" PROPHECIES

To me, when I give somebody a personal prophecy it is a very specific message for them and I like to follow it up afterward. If the Lord gives somebody a direction through a prophetic word, I like to follow it up with practical counsel.

If the Lord says that He is going to release them into prophetic training, I like to follow that up and say, "The

Lord is releasing you as a prophet. This is what you are going to go through. These are the next steps that you are going to have to take now."

Perhaps you give a personal word and the Lord says that He is going to bless their business, or that the road they are on is blocked and He needs them to take a new direction.

When I am finished giving that word, I want to give them some counsel in that direction. I want to tell them the "what, why and where".

Multiple times a day, we get people writing in or contacting us saying, "It was prophesied to me that I am a prophet, but I don't know what to do now." They were just hit with a "drive-by" prophecy!"

Key Principle

> Let's stop the "drive–by prophesying" shall we? Do not rattle off your prophetic word and then run out the door.

Do you know how many times prophets in the Old Testament prophesied over kings and leaders? After each word, they always followed up with counsel and advice.

They delivered their word, and then they said, "The Lord says that you must follow through with this action... "

When Samuel anointed Saul as king, he shared the prophetic word, but then he told him what he needed to do and what was going to happen afterwards. He did not just leave it at that.

From all the examples in the Word, you can see that the personal prophecy can range from being a warning, encouragement or to being a word of judgment. That is why it is vital to share it with the appropriate person.

BECOMING COMFORTABLE WITH PROPHECY

I know that it is time efficient to just call people out in the middle of meetings, but how much affect are you really having? So many leave a meeting like that, thinking, "I was not good enough for the Lord. He had something to say to everyone, except me."

That is why I am a keen advocate of general prophecy. When you make it a habit to share a general prophecy, everyone leaves that meeting feeling as if they heard from the Lord. It helps them to know that God does not play favorites.

Get your categories straight. If the Lord has given you a prophetic word for an individual, share it with them privately. Give them the opportunity to save face. Do not expose their dirty laundry in front of everyone.

You will humiliate them and close any doors for real ministry. On the other hand, if you get a general prophecy, do not be afraid to share it in the group setting. Everyone will be able to revel in the anointing and feel important to God.

As prophets, it is our purpose, at the end of the day, to bring maturity to the Church through a relationship with Jesus. So motivate publically, and prophesy personally, in private. It will set you apart not only as a prophet, but also as a leader others are keen to receive from.

CHAPTER 14

FUNCTIONING IN JOURNALING

Chapter 14 – Functioning in Journaling

> *1 Chronicles 28*
> *19 "All this," said David, "the Lord made me understand in writing, by His hand upon me, all the works of these plans."*

One of the first things that I taught my children when they were old enough, was how to have a conversation. Now, you would think that this is something natural to us humans, but actually I discovered that it wasn't.

A child is not born knowing how to have a good conversation with somebody. In fact, kids usually are very one-sided in their conversation. They are more likely to say, "Look at me!" and to talk about everything they did.

And so, especially being in active ministry and being involved with a lot of people, I had to teach them the social skill of having a conversation. As a mother, I taught them to say things like,

"How are you?"

"You look lovely today!"

"How many children do you have?"

I realized that conversation is really an art. I only saw the fruit of this when they were a little older, and I met somebody who had met the kids at the community swimming pool.

The lady said, "I was so amazed. Your kids showed an interest in the kind of person I am. I never met children like that before. They came into my home and said, 'Wow, you've got such a lovely home. How long have you lived here?'"

She said, "They asked questions that children just never ask and it was such a pleasure to have a conversation with them."

It made me quite a proud mom!

THE "NEEDY PERSON" CONVERSATION

Let's be honest, we all know what it is like to have horrible conversations. You think back about that needy little person – the Lord bless her soul – I know the Lord loves her, but when you see her come towards you, you are looking for another way out.

You know that once she starts, you are going to hear everything that went wrong with her this week; everything that is wrong with her body and everything that she did and didn't do.

It is a horrible conversation and you don't want to talk to this woman because she goes on and on. She doesn't even give you a chance to say anything. Know the type?

The "Well-Intended Advice" Conversation

Or you get those pushy types that never ask you what you want, but tell you what to do all the time! They are so full of well-intended advice.

You can barely say, "I've got a headache," and they say, "You should take this medication," or, "You should see my doctor…"

That is not a very nice conversation either.

A great conversation happens when you have a good friend and the two of you have known each other for a good few years. You have the same interests in the Lord and you can sit down and just talk about your day.

You can just "be" and share what you are going through. A friend like that is someone, that answers with, "I so hate it when that happens! I have been there…"

They are not there to give you counsel or advice. They are not there to tell you what to do. You are just having a good conversation.

The Art of Conversation

You know, these skills are developed - they are not something that we are born with. We learn how to develop communication as we grow up. Now as we come to the subject of journaling, it is very much the same concept.

When I came to training prophets, I assumed that because they could hear the voice of the Lord, that they would naturally know how to journal. As I started our first training courses though, I realized that it was not so natural after all.

There are a lot of preconceived ideas about how to communicate with the Lord.

Where Communication Begins

Most of the skills we learn in how to get along with people, come from the home.

The kind of relationship you had with your parents and siblings, will determine how well you can have a conversation.

So you come to the Lord, ready to share your heart and hear His voice, but find yourself in a bind.

The problem is that you have so many ideas in your mind about how you should be approaching God or how you should be talking to Him, that it starts to hinder your ability to journal.

> **KEY PRINCIPLE**
>
> What is journaling? Simply put, it is a method of conversation via writing whereby you present your thoughts to the Lord, and then write down His answer.

Now, learning how to journal is quite simple and it is a subject that I have already taught on extensively, so I am not going to re-hash that here. Rather, I am going to assume that you know what journaling is and that you have already attempted it.

If you want to get more instruction on how to journal, please read, *The Way of Dreams and Visions, Practical Prophetic Ministry, Called to the Ministry* or *How to Hear the Voice of God*.

DO'S AND DON'TS OF JOURNALING

So in this chapter, I just want to take a look at the do's and don'ts of journaling. They are very practical, so I want you to pick up a pen and paper, or underline them in the book.

Look at each point and ask yourself, "Am I doing that?" or, "Should I not be doing that?" because it is an art.

You know what should be done, but why be satisfied with what you have? There is always place to go deeper!

1. LISTEN

Take the time to hear what God has to say. You might be thinking, "That's a no-brainer - it is journaling after all!" You would be surprised though how many people are so busy talking to the Lord about their problems, that they never stop to hear what He has to say.

Remember how I shared how I taught my children to ask questions and to listen to other people? That is such a vital part of journaling. Listen to what He wants to say. Don't get too self-absorbed.

It could be, that the Lord wants to talk about something completely different. He may want to answer your question in a way you do not expect. I have experienced this many times in my own journals.

I will come to the Lord with a specific topic that I need an answer for. However, when He answers me, it is like he is avoiding the subject!

At times like this, I have to be sensitive to the spirit and realize, "Oh, okay, God wants to talk about something else today."

So you need to come to Him with an open heart. Sure, it is good to come with an idea of what you want to ask the Lord. It is a good place to get started, but don't get stuck there. Get to the point where you say, "Okay Lord, what do you want to say?"

KEY PRINCIPLE

> Some of the best journals I have ever had are when I have come to Him with no agenda and just said, "Lord, what do you want to say to me today? I am open to what you have to say."

Wouldn't it be nice to have a friend that did that for you? That when you hang out together, they say, "What do you have to say? How are you doing? What is on your mind?" and you can offload your heart.

The truth is, this is just not found in today's world. Well, it is not found in many people's relationships with the Lord either. Usually, the conversation is one-sided.

Listen to what God has to say. Really listen. Don't get so wrapped up in your ideas that you do not listen and He has to literally shout to you throughout the journal. Yet no matter how hard the tries, but you keep trying to pull Him back to your point. Don't do it!

2. MAKE YOUR REQUEST CLEAR

The next point is: Make your request clear. When you come to the Lord, come with a clear idea of what you are journaling for. This helps give you a tremendous direction for your journal.

If you just want to hear His voice, then say, "Lord, what do you have to say to me today? What is your direction for me today?"

Come with an idea of what you are going to say, because it is a conversation. Say to the Lord, "Lord, this is my need and care," or, "Hey, how are you doing? I just want to hear what you have to say."

By doing this, it gives you a clear track to run on – a direction for your journal. It is always nice when having a conversation with someone to "get it rolling." Then it can develop from there.

Often though, the Lord will steer off that track or He may not even answer all your questions.

If this happens, don't get stressed about it. He just doesn't want to talk about that right now. He is God - He is allowed to do that. Extend to Him just a little of the grace that He has extended to you.

3. BE REAL AND HONEST

When I am with a good friend, I don't say, "It would please me to have you accompany me, to the nearest coffee shop, so that we might enjoy a tasty beverage together. Would you extend me the grace of accepting my invitation?"

My friends would look at me pretty strangely if I spoke like that! So it stands to reason that I don't talk in theatrical language and religious speech when sharing with someone I know intimately.

I just say, "Hey, how is it going? You want to come around for a cup of coffee?"

Well, Jesus is your best friend and you should be real and honest with Him, more so than with any other person in this world.

I have written so many journals that started out by saying, "Lord, I am having a really bad day, and you know Lord, what that person said really bugged me. Now, I know it shouldn't bug me, but it does! I want to scream and shout!"

Be real. By being honest with the Lord, you let down all your masks – and let's face reality – the Lord knows what is inside of you anyway. He knows that you are ranting, stressed and annoyed anyway.

Scrap the idea, that there is a neat little formula for approaching the Lord. There is no such thing as having to approach the Lord in a formatted, formal way.

Yes, by all means, have a healthy fear of the Father. It is important to have reverence, because He is God.

However, the kind of relationship that I am talking about here is an intimate relationship with the Lord Jesus.

ASK HIM STRAIGHT

When I am intimate with my husband, I do not say, "Would it please you to cometh to the bed - the one whom my soul loves?" ...Not unless I've got some serious issues! My husband would wonder what is up with me!

No, when it is just the two of us, we are real and straightforward with another. It allows us to both just "be" without all the polite overtures. This is what makes life so precious.

The exciting thing is when you are real and honest with Jesus, He is very real and honest back.

Are you looking for a straight answer to something? Then ask Him a straight question. Don't word your question in a way that sounds nicer than the reality - because He knows what's in your heart anyway!

Say it like it is. Say it how you feel it. Say what you are really thinking. Spit it out.

If you feel embarrassed about what you wrote, delete the journal afterwards, okay? (If that makes you feel any better.)

This is a very good starting point to make your journals come alive and to make the Lord feel more real to you.

You get real with Him and you will start to hear some honest answers back.

KEY PRINCIPLE
> When you journal, cut out all the religious "blah blah" and all the stuff that you think you should be doing, and just "be".

Just say, "Lord, you know, I should be reading the Word every day. I should be journaling. I know what I should be doing, but the bottom line is - I don't feel like it."

Boy, are you a sinner! Well, the Lord knows that you are a sinner, but at least you are an honest sinner!

He can deal with that. He can say, "Yes, my child, I know, but you know what, let me show you. Let me teach you."

Then when you are journaling back your response from the Lord, in the same way, allow Him to be honest with you.

Don't try and reword the impressions that come up from your spirit, in veiled speech.

Let Him be honest back to you and I promise you, when you approach the Lord like that, you will be amazed at the clarity of His voice.

4. Do not Paste in Tons of Scriptures

Under no circumstances, should you paste hundreds of scriptures into your journals. What's the point?

That is like having a conversation with a friend, where you try to back up every statement you make, with a scripture.

I hate to break it to you, but the Lord already knows what He said in the Word. He is the one that originated it. He doesn't need to quote it back to Himself.

I see this so often with the prophets. They are journal and then paste the scripture reference in, just to back up what the Lord said.

In fact, the speech of the Word should be natural. When I am teaching, I quote scripture all the time, without having to always give chapter and verse. Do I have to give you "And this is from Matthew 1…"? I don't always need to do it unless I need my audience to make a note of it. Scripture becomes part of my natural speech.

The Language of God

You will find, that as the Lord speaks to you in your journals, He is going to say things like, "My child, I have called you to be the head and not the tail. You are meant to be above and not beneath."

He does not give the disclaimer, "Please go to Deuteronomy 28:44…" He doesn't do it, because He knows where it's found. He spoke it. He originated it. He doesn't need to repeat it and He doesn't need to back Himself up.

Try to get away from it and I will tell you why. If you get into the "I have to go look up all the scriptures" mode, you cut the flow of your spirit and you get into your mind. That is when you start walking a delicate line, that can even lead to deception.

By taking your mind off what God is saying and over analyzing it, you give the enemy the opening he needs to get his ideas in there.

If you are unsure about the content of your journal, then journal first and then go back and look up the scripture afterwards. Yes, the Word is our standard. I am not saying that you shouldn't use the Word as your standard - not at all.

I am just saying, "Stop trying to back every little journal that you receive, with scripture - especially in the middle of a journal!"

Rather let the Word come out of you naturally. Trust me, if you have enough Scripture inside of you, it will bubble out whether you try or not!

If you want to weigh what God said to you against the Word, then you should do that after you are done writing.

PICTURES IN THE WORD

The Lord will use illustrations from the Word all the time. Whether I am in intercession, praying, counseling or journaling, I get illustrations from the Word.

Just like Jesus spoke in parables, He always speaks to me in my journals using pictures. He will say, "This situation you are facing, is like the parable that I told of the ten virgins." Or He will say, "This problem is just like with Lot's wife, when she could not let go…" I don't need to paste in the scripture references.

Those parables in my journals, stand alone and make sense by themselves.

5. DO NOT USE SUPER SPIRITUAL LANGUAGE

From what I have seen over the years, I got the idea that many Christians think that the Lord speaks in King James English.

Here is a newsflash… He doesn't! In fact, you will find that when Jesus walked the earth, He was rather ordinary from your first impression. So much so, that the Pharisees needed Judas to identify Him. He was ordinary looking and ordinary in the language of the day He used.

Of course, the authority, with which He spoke, was something else altogether! There was surely nothing very ordinary about the power with which those words were spoken with!

He spoke in such a way that the uneducated beggars understood Him. Prostitutes understood Him.

When He went to Nicodemus, He had to say, "For somebody that is so learned you are pretty stupid." He was talking so plainly, that Nicodemus in his super-spiritual understanding, could not understand the plainness and the simplicity of His message.

KEY PRINCIPLE

> Don't use super-spiritual language when you journal. Let me tell you a secret – God does not speak that way.

HE TALKS MY LANGUAGE!

When you come into an intimate relationship with Jesus, you will realize that He talks your language. He speaks as you speak. If you speak French, He speaks French. If you speak English, He speaks English. He speaks to you in a way that you will understand Him.

The Lord doesn't speak in high-toned spiritual language all the time and He certainly does not speak in King

James English. He speaks a language that you can understand. He speaks using pictures and types and shadows.

Let me tell you something about Him - He is very, very real. He is very down-to-earth and He is full of power and full of grace, but He also knows how to get His message across.

6. Do Not Use Jargon and Spiritual Buzzwords

I will confess that this is really one of those little hobbyhorses of mine. You know, I can't bear when I see somebody saying, "And I am going to deal with this spirit of divorce and the spirit of abortion... "

I am thinking, "Okay, the spirit of what? Please, could you give me a scripture for that?"

The Lord is not going to say that because it is not in the Word. He is not going to say, "I am going to deal with the spirit of abortion in your life."

Key Principle

> There is no spirit of abortion. There is no spirit of adultery. Let's just call it what is really is – sin!

Having sex with somebody outside of marriage is a sin. It is not a spirit that pounces on you and forces you into submission. It is a sin.

Don't use words and phrases that you have picked up all over the place and then say, "God told this to me in a journal." No, God did not.

God comes up with his own buzzwords.

But you know what the problem is? I realize that there are many "Christian buzzwords" floating around in the Church. There are things that we have grown up with through the years that we believe as if they were Scripture!"

And so you just make them your own. You don't stop to look in the Scripture for yourself. These buzzwords end up becoming a doctrine unto themselves, because no one took the time to look them up in the Word.

So watch out for these little terms, especially common terms that are out there, that are not based on the Word.

Now, you do not need to get paranoid. Sure, there are some good ones that are based on the Word and the Lord will use them to illustrate His point. He will talk about named principles that you have studied, to make a point.

For example, if you have learned about templates, triggers, inner healing or demon manifestations – then

He will use those terms to let you know what principle He is talking about.

Where Did It Originate?

I am going to steal a page out of Apostle Paul's book here and say regarding using buzzwords, "I have no command from the Lord, yet I give my judgment." (1 Corinthians 7:25)

That is just one of my little personal pet peeves and you can take it with a pinch of salt, or you can take it as a challenge and say, "Yes, that's a good point. Why do I always say that? Where did I get that buzzword?

Did I get that from a personal revelation? Did I get that from the Word of God? Or, am I just picking things up from anybody that says something catchy?"

Perhaps you have a few ideas that come to your mind, but here are a few that I often hear.

"New level, new devil."

"Name it and claim it brother!"

"If it's His will, it's His bill!"

"Too blessed to be stressed."

"God is good all the time. All the time, God is good!"

If you want to journal like you never have before, and come into an intimate relationship with the Lord, you need to cut through all the rubbish.

You will need to cut through the religious mindsets. Cut out the fancy language and misconceptions and you will find your relationship with the Lord becoming real, alive and evolving into something beautiful.

Here is a tip to help identify a buzzword – would you use that in an intimate conversation? Remember, I was sharing how conversation is an art.

I am talking about conversations you would have every day of the week and not just on Sundays, when you are around other Christians.

7. Watch Out for Preconceived Ideas

Again, you would be amazed at how much you picked up over the years from different teachings that you just take for granted. We still see the three wise men at the stable, with the shepherds, to worship Jesus.

Reality check… Jesus was nearly two years old when the wise men made it there. I sincerely doubt that they "could not find room at the inn" by the time Jesus reached toddlerhood!

But you know, in my mind I still see the three wise men hanging out with the shepherds in that stable. They are pictures that are just built into our minds and they are not really very accurate.

Key Principle

> When it comes to journaling, you can't put any religious mask on with the Lord. He sees right through you.

Maybe you can get away with it, with other people. In church you can say the "right" words and put on a perfectly pious face. There is no place for it in journaling though.

Stripping the Veils

As a prophet you need to come into a very real, and intimate relationship, with the Lord. That means letting Him strip the veils around your heart.

So, go through your journals. Start saying, "Am I being real here? Am I letting it all hang out?"

When you can let down all the super-spiritual masks and put down all the things that you "should be saying and should be doing", you will touch the heart of the Lord.

You will hear His voice with such clarity, and you will sense His presence like you never have before.

All the masks you have been using to get His attention, will be gone. You can put it down and realize that He has been waiting for you all along, to stop trying to find the right way to approach Him, and to just "be".

Final Challenge

So what are you going to do? Are you going to take up the challenge or are you going to say, "No, my journals are great. I have got it all together. I think it is pretty perfect. "

Is it? Have you developed the art of conversation with the Lord, to the point where you are so comfortable with talking to Him and with hearing what He has to say?

Are your journals still in point form, or do they look like a conversation? They should look as if somebody took the conversation and transcribed it.

If you feel that you are still lacking, then the good news is, that there is always something new to learn. There is so much you still have to discover about the Lord and journaling is a beautiful journey that is meant for you to enjoy. Take your conversation deeper with the Lord, starting today!

CHAPTER 15

FUNCTIONING IN THE AUDIBLE AND STILL SMALL VOICE

Chapter 15 – Functioning in the Audible and Still Small Voice

By now, you are full with so many different ways to hear the Lord. We have the best life in the world as prophets! We get to lose ourselves in the realm of the spirit, and to revel in the secret place with Jesus.

Do you know what I love about Jesus the most? I love that there is always more to know about Him. Just when I think "I have it", He shows me another aspect of His character! So just when you understand prophecy and journaling, there is more to learn!

Without much ado then, let's see how else you can hear from the Lord!

The Audible Voice

> *Acts 22*
> *7 And I fell to the ground and heard a voice saying to me, ' Saul, Saul, why are you persecuting Me?*

Another way to hear the Lord is through the audible voice. This is not as common in the New Testament, but it is certainly the way that Moses must have heard the Lord. You can hear Him audibly as if He was talking out loud in the room. Certainly the evangelist can hear Him in this way.

It is not too common in the prophetic ministry though. Actually, when somebody can only hear the audible voice and doesn't flow in any of the other ways of hearing the Lord, I question it.

I question it a lot, because if they can only hear the audible voice, but don't receive visions, can't journal and can't hear the Lord for themselves, I begin to wonder.

I wonder what voice they are hearing? Is it really the voice of the Lord? If the Lord has to shout all the time, either you do not know how to listen, or the voice you are hearing is not of God, and it is drowning out the still small voice from within.

Key Principle

> God is talking 24 hours a day. You just need to listen.

When I journal, worship, or speak in tongues, I get visions and sense the Urim or Thummim. The moment I get into His presence, the revelation flows automatically.

As a prophet, I can hear God for myself anytime I want. I don't have to wait for "the word" in the form of an audible voice.

So if somebody can only hear an audible voice and doesn't know how to journal or hear the Lord in any other way, I am very suspicious and I want to test that spirit.

So if you wait for the audible voice of God before you feel that you can hear Him, then something is wrong. I would get somebody to judge the spirit on it.

This would fall into the same category as an open vision. Yes, God is well able to speak in this way and He chooses to at times. However, it is not the only way that He speaks to His people.

This holds true even more, of the prophet! If you are called to introduce the Bride to Jesus, it will stand to reason that you can hear Him for yourself. How else will you be able to teach others how to hear Him when they need to?

You cannot tell the Church, that the only way that they can hear God for themselves, is to wait for an audible voice to come from the sky.

I have found that those who have heard an audible voice are those who needed a clear confirmation of their salvation.

It likely happened when they got born-again or it was for the purpose of their salvation. A good example of this, of course, is Apostle Paul on his way to Damascus.

The Lord had to stop him dead in his tracks. Accompanied with that voice was a blinding light and a back-hander, knocking him to the ground!

Fortunately, for us Paul was pretty quick to get the message, and the Lord did not have to resort to such extreme measures again to get through to him!

After that Paul knew with the spirit.

THE STILL SMALL VOICE

> *1 Corinthians 3*
> *16 Do you not know that you are the temple of God and that the Spirit of God dwells in you?*

From the time we are born-again, the Holy Spirit comes to dwell within us. Remember how I taught at the beginning that the Lord speaks to us using our five senses? Well, the still small voice is by far one of the most common ways to hear Him.

In fact, it is likely you have heard this voice often, but just not recognized it. So often we look for the loud voice, not realizing that Jesus is a gentleman.

That is certainly what Elijah experienced when he was running away from Jezebel in 1 Kings 19:12. He expected to hear the Lord in the earthquake, but instead heard Him in the gentle breeze.

This is a beautiful picture of what the Lord had in mind for us all along. As believers, we have the Holy Spirit within and this breeze is always blowing. You will hear it during times when you are crying out for an answer, or when it is time to take a new direction.

How Do You Know if It's God?

When I am feeling weary, He lifts my arms from behind and says, "Push on through. You can do it."

Key Principle

> The still small voice is the Lord speaking to you from your spirit. In fact, it is a lot like receiving a vision - only it is words that are formed in your mind instead of a picture.

It Will Sound Like You

So how do you know if you are making things up or if it is really the Lord? The first time I was aware of this voice, I was sure I was making things up. It happened to me when I met my husband, Craig, for the first time.

We were working as waiters at a popular restaurant, and we bumped into one another on our work shift. As we met, I heard a voice say very clearly in my spirit, "Be careful how you handle this meeting, because this could be your future husband."

I thought I was "hearing things." Well, the Lord knew that I needed a little help, because the road I was determined to walk on at that time, had me going in a very different direction, to the way God wanted me to go!

When you first start paying attention to that inner voice, it starts off with the feeling, of "yes", "no", or "maybe". Then as you develop it more and practice His presence more, you will hear a very soft thought.

It will be a thought that sounds like you, but comes from your spirit.

It will be a thought that says, "I love you."

"I would prefer it, if you did not do that."

"I do not think this is a good idea."

"I really think you should go for that." You may not even be able to vocalize it word for word at the beginning.

IT WILL BE GENTLE

It will be just an array of thoughts, but not pushy thoughts. It will be a gentle thought. Go through the other six ways of hearing His voice before you practice this one.

The enemy will try to put pushy thoughts in your mind. You will need to know the Lord's voice well before listening this way.

You have probably had this already, especially in a crisis, where something happened and you found yourself in a tough or dangerous situation. Suddenly, you had this thought that everything was going to be okay.

It did not even make sense at the time, because in the natural, everything was falling apart. The bills were due, the finances were not coming in, but you had this thought in your mind that everything would be okay and that the rent would be paid.

You thought, "Where did that thought come from?"

When you start realizing that those thoughts are the voice of the Lord, and you link them to the Urim and Thummim and to the Word you have been pushing down, guess what happens?

Pictures start to build. You realize that God has been trying to tell you something all along. That is the wonderful thing about hearing the Lord's voice.

He does not speak in just one way. He does not give you a prophetic word, and that is it.

He will speak through the Urim and Thummim, visions and then in your journal.

SPIRITUAL MATURITY

It is a sign of spiritual maturity if you hear His voice without Him having to shout from the heavens.

Perhaps you have already noticed that there is a definite progression when it comes to hearing God's voice. In fact, if you look over your spiritual life from the time you got saved, to the point you are at now – things have changed a lot.

There is a progression in the way you have heard Him through the years. The first time you heard His voice it was like the heavens opened, and the ground shook!

The first time the Lord wants you to bring a word or wants you to know His will, you get that "butterfly" feeling in your stomach. It feels like a knot, and along with it you feel a surge of anointing.

The anointing is so strong and you feel the power of God. Some people have a physical manifestation or hear God even audibly.

When you flow for the first time in a spiritual gift, the chances are that the feelings and impressions you received, were very strong!

This was a fantastic start along this road. God got your attention. What you will find though as you mature spiritually, is that this way of hearing God changes. A progression takes place.

THE PROGRESSION

It is like I already shared about Elijah. He went from having God answer with fire from heaven, to having to listen intently as He spoke through a very gentle breeze.

This is what you are going to experience as you come to hear the voice of God. You will realize that it does not always have to be a ground shaking experience.

Perhaps you have been feeling a bit "less of a prophet" lately. The first time you got a vision or a prophetic word, you felt a powerful anointing. You experienced such power that your hands shook. You felt it over your whole body!

However, over time, it stopped and you thought, "I really missed it. I guess God is not as present with me these days. I must have lost something".

No, you didn't miss it. Guess what? You are growing up!

Key Principle

> The ability to hear the gentle voice of Jesus indicates someone who has his ear so closely pressed to the heart of the Father, that he can hear every murmur.

Sometimes my husband wants to tell me something that he doesn't want the whole world to hear. We will be in public and he will come up behind me and whisper something in my ear.

All he needs to do to get my attention, is to come to my side, and to whisper something in my ear. He doesn't have to stand on the other end of the room and shout at me.

I know the sound of his voice, I know his accent and I know the way that he is going to speak to me. Well, it is the same with the Lord.

Perhaps when you first started flowing in the gifts, you couldn't hear Him so well, so He had to shout. You needed the anointing or the manifestation as a confirmation.

Sometimes you were not aware that He was speaking, so He had to talk louder than usual to get your attention. However, you have come to know the Lord. He has your attention now, and He doesn't need to keep shouting. You are growing up! You are now headed for a very precious time of intimacy with Jesus.

CHAPTER 16

THE SIGN OF TRUE INTIMACY

Chapter 16 – The Sign of True Intimacy

You know, I would worry if my husband would always have to shout at me to get my attention. It would be a good indication that I was either hard of hearing, or that I did not give him the time of day.

The time will come as you develop these different ways of hearing God, that instead of many manifestations, you will feel the gentle nudging of the Spirit instead.

You will come to such an intimate relationship with Jesus, that you will just know what He wants. You will not need a super-duper experience to sense Him nearby.

You will experience Him the most through seasons of rest. He will come up to you and whisper tenderly into your ear, and you will know, "Yes, that's the Lord."

This gentle voice is the true nature of the Lord Jesus. His voice is like a gentle breeze that blows over barren land, transforming it from death to life.

The Essence of God

This is the essence of His nature. He brings peace, He brings joy, He brings rest - He doesn't always need to shake you.

Learn to develop all of the seven ways to hear the Lord, always keeping the goal in your mind, to hear that still small voice. Make it your goal to be sensitive enough to pay attention to the urgings deep inside.

Know Him so well, that your ears prick up the moment you feel that little rumbling deep inside that says, "I am speaking to you now."

As you get to know the nature of the Lord, you will come to the place where you will not always have to find a quiet place to hear Him.

You will find that you will not need to spend hours in His presence just to get a single direction. Instead of taking hours to hear for yourself, you will be able to use that time to fill up and pour out to others.

You will realize that you don't have to wait for hours and tarry in the spirit to hear Him. Soon He will be so real to you that you will be able to hear Him even when you are in the middle of doing something.

I can be running around, doing a hundred things all at once, yet no matter how busy I am, I can still hear the sound of my husband's voice, even if he calls me from the other side of the house.

The tremor of his voice resonates in my ears, and they prick up to follow it. It is the same with the Lord.

You can be at work - piled over with contracts. The phone could be ringing off the hook, and He will be able to tap you on the shoulder and your ears will prick up.

"Yes, Lord?"

Now that's a sign of maturity and that's what we are going to aim for as we start coming to the end of this book.

THE LOVE RELATIONSHIP

When you come to the place, when you're walking in an intimate relationship with the Lord Jesus, all the gifts and receiving of revelation will fall into line.

Paul gets us all fired up about the gifts of the Spirit in 1 Corinthians 12, only to end on the strangest low note. After ranting about how all of us have a place and how the Holy Spirit manifests the gifts through us, He ends by saying, "…but let me show you a better way."

Chapter 13 is the better way. It is the chapter on love.

As you come into this relationship with Jesus, you will finally understand the passage:

> *1 Corinthians 13*
> *8 Love never fails. But whether there are prophecies, they will fail; whether there are tongues, they will cease; whether there is knowledge, it will vanish away.*

KEY PRINCIPLE

> The purpose of being able to hear God's voice is not being able to prophesy or "get revelation." Rather, the point of it all is to come into the perfect knowledge of His agape love.

It is only in the presence of Jesus that you will experience this love. It is only through hearing His voice, for yourself that you will not only feel, but be able to pour out with this love.

THE PURPOSE FOR HEARING HIS VOICE

Have you noticed how easily people rub off on you? You make a new friend, and before you know it, you are using phrases that they use. It is quite the thing in our ministry. Because we are so international, we have rubbed off on each other so much so, that you can hear a whole variety of phrases around the dinner table.

Someone will ask for the salt in German, another will answer in Spanish, as someone throws out a typical American English slang.

You will notice that each church and community, has a certain language of their own. You find your mindsets and likes being influenced by those around you. It is the way the Lord created us. He created us to connect with those around us.

Well, imagine for a moment that the Lord was the one doing most of the "rubbing off" on you.

How is this going to happen? The only way it can take place, is when you put yourself in a place to hear His voice often. Soon you will find yourself using His catch phrases.

You will find His agape love rubbing off on you. Soon your walk with Him will not be about "gifts" and "revelations", but completely about relationship.

When you get to that point, then you have something to hand out to the body of Christ.

EXPERIENCE HIM WITH ALL 5 SENSES!

So do not limit yourself! In these 16 Chapters, I have taught you different ways to hear His voice, but actually, I have taught you on how to hear, see, feel, smell and taste His voice!

I have taught you to be sensitive to the messages that are coming from your spirit all of the time. Now imagine that you can combine them all.

Give it a try next time you are in His presence. Try to involve all your sense, in hearing Him.

When you come to the Lord to receive direction – whether it is through prayer or journaling, be mindful of the following things:

1. What visions am I seeing? What pictures are coming up in my mind right now?
2. What sounds am I hearing right now? Do I hear words or a specific sound?
3. What do I feel inside of me right now? Urim? Thummim? Warning? Joy?
4. What do I smell in the spirit? Am I aware of a fragrance?
5. What do I taste in the spirit right now? Is there something "sweet in the air?"

Give it a try! By doing it, you allow yourself to experience the Lord in His fullness. It means that you will be completely engaged with Him. It will not be long at all and the nature of the Lord will begin to show in you.

You see that is what the fruit of the Spirit is all about. Have you ever wondered how to develop the fruit of the Spirit in your life? Well, this is the secret. Experience Jesus!

The more you are wrapped up in Him, the quicker you will pick up His nature and along with that, every fruit of the Spirit. This is the natural progression of not just the prophet, but of every believer.

However, before you can claim yourself the "expert on hearing God", it is a good idea to learn every way of how to hear His voice.

By this stage of your journey, you will come to realize that it has become a lot more than just "hearing His voice" but about "becoming the image of Christ."

With that revelation, you are fast on your way to fulfilling your function as a prophet.

ABOUT THE AUTHOR

Born in Bulawayo, Zimbabwe and raised in South Africa, Colette had a zeal to serve the Lord from a young age. Coming from a long line of Christian leaders and having grown up as a pastor's kid she is no stranger to the realities of ministry. Despite having to endure many hardships such as her parent's divorce, rejection, and poverty, she continues to follow after the Lord passionately. Overcoming these obstacles early in her life has built a foundation of compassion and desire to help others gain victory in their lives.

Since then, the Lord has led Colette, with her husband Craig Toach, to establish *Apostolic Movement International,* a ministry to train and minister to Christian leaders all over the world, where they share all the wisdom that the Lord has given them through each and every time they chose to walk through the refining fire in their personal lives, as well as in ministry.

In addition, Colette is a fantastic cook, an amazing mom to not only her 4 natural children, but to her numerous spiritual children all over the world. Colette is also a renowned author, mentor, trainer and a woman that has great taste in shoes! The scripture to "be all things to all men" definitely applies here, and the Lord keeps adding to that list of things each and every day.

How does she do it all? Page through every book and teaching to experience the life of an apostle firsthand and get the insight into how the call of God can make every aspect of your life an incredible adventure.

Read more at www.colette-toach.com

Connect with Colette Toach on Facebook! www.facebook.com/ColetteToach

RECOMMENDATIONS BY THE AUTHOR

If you enjoyed this book, we know you will also love the following books on the prophetic.

PROPHETIC ANOINTING

Book 3 of the Prophetic Field Guide Series

By Colette Toach

God has promised you a visit to the throne room! This is your summons from Almighty God. It is time for you to experience Him face-to-face and heart-to-heart.

Get ready for the meeting of a lifetime. The veils that have hindered the anointing in your life are going to be ripped away, and you are going to shine with His glory in every area of your life.

PRESENTATION OF PROPHECY

By Colette Toach

You do not need to be a prophet to prophecy and God will not come forcibly on you and make you do anything.

It is indeed a gift of the spirit that can be practiced. By the end of this book, you will be amazed to discover how accessible this gift of the Holy Spirit is to you. You will know the steps 1, 2, 3 of presenting prophecy.

I'M NOT CRAZY - I'M A PROPHET

By Colette Toach

It takes a prophet to know a prophet! You do not have to follow in the footsteps of others before you take the wealth of this book and rise above the pit falls.

That is why only Colette Toach can take the prophetic and dish it out in its truth and cover the subjects included in this book. So are you crazy? Maybe a little, but this book will help you to be the true prophet that God has called you to be!

THE WAY OF DREAMS & VISIONS BOOK WITH SYMBOL DICTIONARY KIT

By Colette Toach

 +

In this kit you are not only getting the teaching you need to understand your dreams and visions, but you are also getting the key to decode them.

Everybody wants to Interpret Dreams today. But where is the balance between what the world says and what the WORD says? You are about to find out that as a believer, there is a world in the spirit and in the word that breaks all the boundaries of what you knew - or thought you knew.

PRACTICAL PROPHETIC MINISTRY

By Colette Toach

Wouldn't it be incredible if someone could have walked you through your prophetic calling and pointed out all the potholes before you fell into them?

Unfolded step by step, you will have someone along the way telling you what to avoid, what to embrace and most importantly... what to do next along your prophetic journey.

PROPHETIC ESSENTIALS

Book 1 of the Prophetic Field Guide Series

By Colette Toach

In this book, you will find out that the call of the prophet goes far deeper than the functions and duties that the prophet fulfills. Anyone flowing in prophetic ministry can carry out tasks similar to the prophet.

If it burns in you to pay any price that is necessary and to stand up and break down the barriers between the Lord Jesus and His Bride, then my friend, you have picked up the right tool that will confirm the fire in your belly and the call of God on your life.

A.M.I. Prophetic School

www.prophetic-school.com

Whether you are just starting out or have been along the way for some time, we all have questions.

Who better to answer them than another prophet!

With over 18 years of experience, the A.M.I. Prophetic School is the leader in the prophetic realm.

From dedicated lecturers to live streaming and graduation, the A.M.I. Prophetic School is your home away from home.

What Our Prophetic Training Accomplishes

Our extensive training is a full two-year curriculum that will:

1. Identify and confirm your prophetic call
2. Effectively train you to flow in all the gifts of the Spirit
3. Fulfill your purpose as a prophet in the local church
4. Take your hand through the prophetic training process
5. Specialist training in spiritual warfare
6. Arm you for intercession and decree
7. Minister in praise and worship
8. Achieve prophetic maturity

CONTACT INFORMATION

To check out our wide selection of materials, got to:
www.ami-bookshop.com

Do you have any questions about any products?

Contact us at: +1 (760) 466 - 7679
(8am to 5pm California Time, Weekdays Only)

E-mail Address: admin@ami-bookshop.com

Postal Address:

>A.M.I
>5663 Balboa Ave #416
>San Diego, CA 92111, USA

Facebook Page:
http://www.facebook.com/ApostolicMovementInternational

YouTube Page:
https://www.youtube.com/c/ApostolicMovementInternational

Twitter Page: https://twitter.com/apmoveint

AMI Bookshop – It's not Just Knowledge, It's **Living Knowledge**

www.ingramcontent.com/pod-product-compliance
Lightning Source LLC
Chambersburg PA
CBHW070641160426
43194CB00009B/1533